EXCUSE
LIMIT
ZERO

HOW TO OVERCOME
YOUR MISTAKES &
THRIVE

GREGORY FERNANDES

Excuse Limit Zero: How to Overcome Your Mistakes and Thrive
By Gregory Fernandes

Published by

Brockton, MA

ISBN: 978-0-578-61970-5

Personal Memoir

Cover and Interior design by Nick Zelinger of NZ Graphics

QUANTITY PURCHASES: Schools, companies, professional groups,
clubs, and other organizations may qualify for special terms
when ordering quantities of this title. For information, email
info@treblebasspublishing.com.

Printed in the United States of America

First Edition

CONTENTS

Foreword 5

Prologue 9

PART 1: My Story 13

1: One Foot on the Banana Peel 15

2: From Freedom to Rock and Roll 42

3: Hitting Rock Bottom 62

PART 2: The Lessons 81

4: Embrace the F*ck Up 83

5: Only Complain When It Counts 101

6: Use Everything 123

7: Reimagine Yourself 138

Acknowledgments: My Mount Rushmore 153

About the Author 161

FOREWORD

"Did you call Greg?"

"No, Dad, he called me a couple times, but I've been too busy."

"Steve, I want you to call him! He's the son of my colleague and I've known him since he was a little boy. He's a talented kid and he's looking for work."

"Okay, Dad."

The following week:

"Steve, did you call him?"

Sigh.

"CALL HIM!"

Greg Fernandes was in my office that afternoon in October 2004. My DJ company had just lost a key party emcee and I was in search of a replacement. Within five minutes of meeting Greg, I knew G-d had sent me an angel! Greg's dream was to be an entertainer, and I needed an entertainer.

"Come to my party tonight," I said.

"I'll be there."

"Wear black."

"Yes, sir."

When I put that microphone in his hand five hours later, I knew we were a match made in heaven. What I didn't know was that Greg and I were destined to become lifelong friends, and that I would grow to care deeply for him. Although we come from completely different sides of the track, it is me he calls in times of crisis and confusion. When I get the call, I take a deep breath and guide Greg as if he were my own son. I am a Jewish white guy from Newton, Massachusetts. What binds us so deeply together? Our mutual love of music and our two beloved deceased parents, my dad and his mom, who taught music side by side at the Boston Latin School for over fifteen years, may they rest in peace.

When you befriend someone who has experienced the hardships that Greg describes in this book, you had better buckle up, because you will ride on their roller coaster with them. I wouldn't trade the ride you are about to read for anything in the world. This middle-aged entrepreneur has learned more from Greg than I ever taught him. This is a memoir about a boy of mixed color "too light-skinned to fit in with the black kids, and too dark-skinned to fit in with the white kids." He loved to play the violin but struggled to be accepted by his elementary school classmates. Greg's journey from a promising young musician to drug dealer and prison inmate, and then reemerging to become an elite party emcee and one of the most incredible teachers on the planet is frankly hard to believe, but it's true.

As a young Cape Verdean, Greg feared for his life as he walked down the hallway of his middle school clutching his violin case. In a racially divided town, where he fit in with no race, he feared that he could get jumped and beat up at any moment. To survive, he would need to give the impression that he was a "tough guy" able to defend himself in a fist fight, and selling weed in the school yard. The truth was that Greg got through each day feeling scared, weak, and alone, which led him into a tumultuous adolescence. Fists became knives and weed became crack. Greg carries these scars from his youth wherever he goes, but he makes ZERO excuses.

When his mom died suddenly in June of 2010, Greg hit "rock bottom," and says his "anger and frustration felt unbearable." The only way he could numb the intense emotional pain was through drugs and alcohol. It was at this time that he realized his life was in peril and only he could save it. He checked himself into a detox program. Greg was about to take control of his life once and for all.

With a healthy mind and body and a fresh perspective on life, Greg pursued his dream of teaching music to children, and realized it. Following in the footsteps of his mother, he became the music director of a renowned private school. Greg vividly explains two racially motivated incidences that occurred recently in his life. In the first, he is surrounded by Boston police officers in the train station, and in the second, he is unjustly fired from the aforementioned "dream job." Both situations threatened to derail him and rocked him to the core, but THIS time Greg walked away and landed himself another job just as prestigious as his last. Why? Because he is everything his mother ever believed he would be, and now he finally knows it!

In his book, Greg demonstrates that bad choices do not define us; they can be a springboard for change. Greg's important life lessons will motivate you to take action in your own life.

If a young Cape Verdean boy who served jail time for dealing drugs can achieve his dream of being a music educator at one of the most prestigious private schools in the country, you can live your dream too.

Greg teaches us that YOU control your destiny. "You're better than your bad decisions," so embrace your present and never give up on your dreams. Most importantly, don't make excuses for why your life is the way it is, because the Excuse Limit is . . . Zero.

—Steven Siagel, President and CEO
of Siagel Productions Inc.

PROLOGUE

I have a sign that hangs in my music classroom that reads, "Excuse Limit Zero." I point to it when my students complain about an exercise or a piece of music being too hard, when they leave an instrument at home, when they give me excuses about why they couldn't practice, or when they come in talking about how they're going to give up on themselves—in music or in life. For me, it represents everything—all the ecstatic joy in my life and all the extreme sadness I've experienced, and the mindset that allowed me to get through it all. This is why a simple phrase on a poster became the foundation of this book.

Because the truth is, I've had to overcome a huge amount of adversity in my life. I'm currently working in my dream job as a music teacher at one of the most elite schools in the United States, and, in my free time, I get to experience truly incredible moments with wonderful people, and explore the most picturesque of cities. But the years that led up to now have also been lined with harrowing snippets of self-destructive behavior. That's why I want to share this story.

For many people, especially people of color, it's hard to fully understand that your mistakes and bad decisions do not define you. No matter who you are, or what race or background you come from, if you can accept the decisions you've made and learn to move past any regret you feel toward them, you can become better than your bad decisions. If you try your best to make first-rate decisions for yourself at any current point in time, you're better than your bad decisions. And even if you screw up sometimes, you're still better than your bad decisions. I refuse to believe that any of us are awful just because we have made some bad choices in the past. If we are working toward becoming better versions of ourselves, one bad judgement won't change that. The bad decisions in your past don't make you a bad person. While they are a part of you and who you were at the time, they don't define who you are now. Your bad decisions make you human. And you're probably going to make a ton more.

I want you to feel what I feel. I want you to experience my experiences for yourself. You see, I don't want to forget any of it, whether the stories are about the good, bad, or ugly. I've documented these moments on paper over the last six months, and I hope you will find honesty, credibility, and inspiration in my words. A problem shared is a problem halved, right?

This is not a how-to book; it is a collection of life stories and experiences, and a little insight that I hope might, in some way, help you.

My goal for the book is to pass along the priceless lessons I've absorbed over the years. Some of the lessons I've discovered on my own. Others have been passed down by wise elders, both in my family and those I've been fortunate enough to meet. Regardless of their origin, I hope you'll find value here.

In short, this book is about how I went from having, as my father would always say, "one foot on a banana peel, one foot in jail, and my third leg in a grave," to figuring out how to get my feet back beneath me and set in the right direction. And how it all started when I set my personal excuse limit to ZERO.

PART 1
My Story

1

ONE FOOT ON THE BANANA PEEL

*"True happiness . . . is not attained through
self-gratification, but through fidelity
to a worthy purpose."*
~ Helen Keller

I was the worst drug dealer ever. For that matter, I wasn't good at any of the gangster shit that I did. I smoked all of the weed I tried to sell, the one time I brought a gun to school (unloaded) I had to ditch it before I could use it, and I only lasted a couple of months selling crack before I got busted.

The truth is, I wasn't cut out to be a gangster. I went out of my way to make people think I was, but it wasn't natural for me. It just wasn't how I was raised. My dad was a laborer, a hard worker with an endless array of side gigs, and my mother had a master's degree in music and taught at one of the most elite public schools in the world:

Boston Latin School. Between their two incomes, we were firmly middle class. They went out of their way to keep me from resorting to crime and violence, and it must have worked, because though I drifted down that path, I never became fully unmoored.

My parents' made their first major change to keep me on the straight and narrow a year before I was born. They knew they wanted kids, and they realized that the only places in Boston proper where they could afford to live were overrun with crime and violence. They wanted to shelter us from all of that, so they moved out to Brockton, about thirty minutes south of Boston. It was once a prosperous town, and back in the late 1800s, Brockton was America's largest producer of shoes. Up until the latter parts of the twentieth century, Brockton had a large shoe and leather products industry.

At the time we moved there, Brockton was still very segregated, and we moved into the black part of town. My parents traded the traffic, noise, chaos, and apartment buildings of the inner city for the quiet and spaciousness of real houses in the burbs. The move was a significant step up from the mean streets of Roxbury in Boston.

By the time I turned seven, my parents had become a power couple, and they decided to have their first house built in the white part of town. We were the only black family in the area. It only took three weeks for someone to spray paint "Go Away Nigers" on the garage. If it so much as made my parents bat an eye, they hid it from my younger siblings and me. For the longest time, the running joke was that whatever idiot did it was so stupid, they couldn't even spell "Niggers" correctly.

Growing up in that area, I didn't even realize we were upper-middle class. Until I became much older, I thought everyone had both parents around every day, a treehouse, a pool, multiple vehicles, and plenty of food. While we knew that our mother had grown up poor, we had no idea of what that actually meant. She kept it far away from us, so we never understood all that we had by comparison.

The schools in the area weren't too bad, and I went to Brockton Public Schools until third grade. But my mom had a plan for her eldest, and that plan included Boston Latin School. And if you wanted to go to BLS, you'd better go to a good elementary school. So, when I was in fourth grade, my mom put me in a private school called Parkside Elementary in Jamaica Plain, a borough of Boston. My sisters stayed in Brockton Public Schools. Deanna, the youngest, was still a baby at the time, and my other sister Ty, a year and a half younger than me, was super smart, super focused, and thriving in the Brockton Public School system. I simply needed more attention to help me focus.

Parkside Elementary was on my mom's way to work, so I had the honor of riding with my mom every day. I loved spending time with her. Each morning, while listening to Lauren and Wally on 105.7, sometimes Magic 106.7, Boston's soft rock station, she would drill me on my spelling words and make me read. Of course, this was all early in the morning, so sometimes I would try to catch extra sleep by making it look like I was reading with my head down. She caught me almost every time and would yell, "Wake up!"

My mother and I shared a very special bond. Maybe it was because I was her firstborn, maybe it was because I looked like her birth father, or maybe it was the music. Whatever it was, our bond was unique.

Her plan worked: after Parkside Elementary, I passed the notoriously difficult entrance exam and got into Boston Latin school. The test was known to be hard, and I remember being sweaty and shaky when I took it, but I knew I'd get in: I was Mrs. Fernandes's kid.

If the test to get in was hard, it was nothing compared to the school itself. BLS is legendary for the amount of pressure they put on students, and I didn't respond to the pressure well. I didn't apply myself to my studies, and I channeled my energy into antics instead. I got suspended a couple of times but not for anything serious. Just dumb stuff, like jumping out of the first-floor window of the English classroom and running back upstairs to the classroom before the teacher got there.

For all of my academic and behavioral problems, I always thrived in music. This made sense—violin had been at the forefront of my life since I was three years old. While I was a ten-year-old at Parkside Elementary, my mom would arrange for an upperclassman from BLS to pick me up after school and take me to BLS so I could rehearse with the high school orchestra led by Lou Siagel. I would sit in the first violin chair, next to the best violin player in the whole school, and my legs couldn't even reach the floor. I was that good. Because of this, I knew the director of the orchestra department, Mr. Siagel, for years before I attended BLS as a student.

My mother's classroom and his classroom were fifteen feet apart, so whenever my sisters and I would visit BLS, we would run between the two rooms. We loved Mr. Siagel, and he loved us—so much so that I thought of him as a sort of unofficial uncle. It helped that, for a long time, I had believed Mr. Siagel was black. He had very curly, almost nappy, coarse hair. His skin was brown and, more than anything, he had soul. Eventually, I discovered Mr. Siagel was Jewish, not black.

At BLS, where everything was a challenge, I took pride in my performance in Mr. Siagel's orchestra. He gave me private instruction, encouraged me with enthusiasm, and made me a beast on the violin. The competition was fierce, both educationally and musically, but I had been a star student of his before I'd even enrolled. It helped that Mr. Siagel treated me like a son. He even stood by me for years after I left—I still have the letter of recommendation he wrote for me in seventh grade when I applied to an elite violin program run by the Boston Symphony Orchestra.

As well as I did in music, my performance in other areas was dangerously bad. My mother did everything she could to help. She hired tutors, she talked to my teachers (her co-workers) and tried to get me extra time and extra attention. She even drove me to the Latin teacher's house on Saturdays for extra lessons.

It didn't work. After two years of horrible grades, my mother broke the news to me: I was no longer allowed to attend BLS. BLS is a public school; therefore, you had to live in Boston to attend. Had I been a stellar student, I suspect they may have overlooked the fact that we didn't live in Boston, but since I was a pain in the ass and my grades were terrible, when the school discovered that we lived in Brockton, the loophole of the residency requirement was an easy way to get me to leave without losing my mother as their music teacher. So the decision was made. I would attend Brockton High School at the beginning of my ninth-grade year.

I had one friend in Brockton, Sean Corcoran. He lived across the street, and when we moved to the new house, he was the first kid I met. I was seven. Sean was white, my age, and had three much older siblings. Sean and I did everything together until seventh grade.

Once we entered seventh grade, at different schools, of course, that's when real life kicked in. That's when Sean and I realized that he was white, and I was black. We'd been best friends for five years prior, but our racial difference had never been an issue or even discussed. Sean had a new group of friends from his middle school, who were all white. Every day after school, when Sean and I would meet up, I never felt comfortable around any of them, so our relationship began to fade. There are lots of elementary schools in Brockton, but at that time, there were only four middle schools, North, South, East, and West. What that means is that every kid in Brockton went to one of these four middle schools, so whether it was through sports, arts, or academics, the students in the middle schools connected.

By the time you got to high school, you pretty much knew everyone who would be in your class. I, on the other hand, didn't know anybody. Before the first day of high school, my mother and I met with a guidance counselor from Brockton High. He asked how I was feeling about the transition, and I told him that I was scared to ride the bus to school with a bunch of people I didn't know. Instead, I said, I'd ride my bike—I only lived about a mile away from school. The guidance counselor just shook his head and said, "Honestly, if you bring your bike and chain it up outside, when you leave school, it'll be gone." He went on to tell me that, when I was in school, I needed to make sure I walked with someone.

I left the meeting feeling worse about the transition than I did going into it. Even though he still lived in the neighborhood, my old friend Sean went to the local Catholic high school, Cardinal Spellman, so as far as I was concerned, I didn't know anyone in Brockton.

More than feeling like I was headed for high school, I felt like I was on my way to a juvenile detention center. In spite of this, my mother hoped that I would fit in. She knew the head of the music department and the choral director at Brockton High, and she arranged for me to go in and play the violin for them during the first week of school, to see if they could fit me in a band or some other musical ensemble.

Brockton High School was not the sort of place where you wanted to be seen with a violin.

The kids were just plain fucked up to me because of it. I heard a few rumors that a group of guys were saying things like, "He thinks he's fucking special because he lives in a nice house and plays the violin. Uppity ass nigga."

From that point on, I was on high alert. The routes I walked to class were all planned. One day, I feared for my life when I thought I was about to get jumped. Often, when I saw certain people coming, I would hide. I would sometimes find a place to hide for an hour after school, just so I wouldn't bump into anyone during the wild exit at 2:00 p.m. I also told my mom that if she wanted me to bring my violin to school, then she would have to drop it off to the music room because I was not going to carry it anymore. That didn't happen, and it wasn't long before the violin was no longer part of my life.

Even without the violin, I knew I wouldn't last long without music in my life. One of the people my mom knew at the school was Vincent Macrina, the head of the Brockton High music department. He used to come around with his brass band to our church for Easter or Christmas services, so he was aware of who I was. Vincent

Macrina was a man with a vision. Vinny was well known for his amazing marching band, and he wanted me to be the main attraction. The day of our first meeting, he told me he wanted me to take up the tuba. He thought that it would be something special—the smallest guy in school, playing the biggest instrument.

I wasn't interested in joining his band, or in being the butt of what felt like some weird joke. Besides, I didn't want to learn the tuba. The violin was my instrument, and since that wasn't an option, I decided to join the chorus instead. You don't get beaten up for walking around with your voice.

Vinny was not happy about this at all, to say the least. Because of how impressive his band shows were, he was something of a big deal in the school, and he wasn't used to people saying no to him. From the moment I refused to take up the tuba, I could tell that I had offended him. Lucky me. Within the first couple of weeks at this brand new school where I feared for my life, I made the head of the music department my arch enemy.

Now I was the chorus guy. I had completely abandoned the violin and any other instrument. My mom begged me not to throw away something I was so good at, but I wouldn't be swayed. As usual, she let me make my own decision. I'm sure she was aware of the huge dilemma I was facing with the kids at school, but there was nothing she could do to save her baby. I was young. The outside world had already made me hate myself and try to hide who I really was. I was too light-skinned to fit in with the black kids, and I was too dark-skinned to fit in with the white kids. I felt completely insignificant. I went from being the little superstar in Mr. Siagel's orchestra to a target of ridicule.

This was the point of my life when I perfected the art of a dual personality. I found a way to express myself musically, and I made lots of friends in chorus. But I still had no real friends. In the eyes of the student body, I couldn't hang with chorus kids outside of the chorus room. Other students looked at the chorus kids as the nerdy, uncool kids—everything I did not want to be.

This was one of the many segregating divisions in Brockton High. You had the Haitians, Jamaicans, the Cape Verdeans, the whites, the blacks, and "the others," which refers to the kids who flew under the radar—the kids that had mastered the art of being invisible in a sea of rogue sharks.

At lunch, you sat with your people. During off periods, you sat with your people. You walked home with your people, played basketball with your people after school or on the weekends. So that's what I did. I latched on to the first group of African Americans that accepted me. Granted, I'm half Cape Verdean, but the Cape Verdeans never fully accepted me because I didn't speak the language. After that, it wasn't hard for me to make friends. In some ways, I lead more than a double life, a triple, or even quadruple life. I had my chorus friends, my African

American friends, but I also managed to get in good with the Jamaicans, the Haitians, and the white kids. I always knew at least one person in any group I encountered, and, in many ways, this kept me safe in and out of school.

       ※ ※ ※ ※

When I arrived at Brockton High, I hadn't known a single person. Just a couple of years later, I was so well known and liked that I was one of the few people who could walk the streets of Brockton at any time of the night and not be worried.

But back to my multilayered life. I was a member of the concert choir, the jazz choir, the show choir, and drama— and lived like it. I always had rehearsals, concerts, festivals, and performances. This meant that I would hardly see or spend any time with my "inner" city friends, just a couple of free hours here or there. Despite the arts taking up most of my time, I kept my singing and drama commitments hidden from my city friends, to the point where there are people who still have no idea I sang during high school. When I run into any of them and tell them that I'm a music teacher now, they can't believe it.

Likewise, my chorus friends probably wouldn't believe the kind of nonsense I got myself into during high school. I tried to sell weed a couple of times, buying an ounce and splitting it into dime bags, then hawking it in the schoolyard. Fortunately, I never got good enough at it to draw attention to myself—more often than not, I'd smoke all of my own weed before I could sell it. I also picked up a couple of minor arrests in high school for things like fighting or threatening to beat someone up. I wanted everyone to think I was a gangster, and that I was a lot tougher than I truly was, even though I went home and practiced Handel every night.

Despite my relatively compliant behavior at home, my father was wise to my antics, and he used to warn me that I had "one foot on the banana peel," and I had better watch my step.

To that end, I did a lot of stupid stuff with my friends. We used to break into houses and steal the little crystals off of chandeliers because we thought they were diamonds. I got stabbed a couple of times in high school, once during a Brockton tradition, the "Birthday Beat Down," where a group of guys would get together to kick the shit out of one of their poor friends who happened to have a birthday. We went to surround a friend of mine on his birthday. There were about fifteen of us, and he knew what was up right away, so he pulled a knife and said he'd cut whoever tried to give him a beat down. Well, there were fifteen of us, and none of us wanted to look scared, so we jumped him anyway. I happened to catch some of the knife.

Perhaps my stupidest attempt to act like a gangster started with a girl: Nidia. Nidia and I had dated at the end of my freshman year and into my sophomore year, then she broke up with me, and she took up with a guy named

Nick. Only, Nidia and I kept fooling around on the side. One day, at the end of school, I was getting my stuff from my locker, when Nick and about four of his friends came toward me. In Brockton High, each block of lockers is set off from the main hallway in a giant U, with the only entrance or exit at the top of the U. My locker was at the bottom of the U, and as Nick and his boys came toward me, they spread out to block my means of escape.

It so happened that Nick had found out about Nidia and me. He told me he was going to kick my ass. I was quick and strong and no stranger to fights, but I was also small, cornered, and outnumbered five to one. I don't remember exactly how it happened, but I escaped, by some miracle, unscathed.

When I got home, I was pissed off, and I knew that I didn't want Nick and his guys on my ass for the rest of high school. So I came up with a plan, which, at the time, seemed brilliant. That night, I got a pistol from a friend. The next morning, I made sure it wasn't loaded, and I brought it to school.

My plan was to corner Nick in the bathroom, pull the gun on him, scare the shit out of him, and then return the gun to its owner. The plan was stupid, but I made an even stupider mistake that day: right when I got to the bus stop, I showed the gun to one of my buddies and told him what I was planning on doing. Obviously, I was never cut out for the gangster life. Later that day, I was walking through the hallway, gun shoved in my belt, and looking for Nick so I could tail him into a bathroom or something, when I bumped into a girl I hardly knew.

"Greg," she said, "I don't know what the hell you've done, but I was just in the office and the only thing any of them can say is 'Greg Fernandes.'"

I, of course, knew exactly what they were talking about. Somebody, maybe my friend or someone who overheard us, must have told a teacher about the gun. I thanked this person and ran to a different buddy of mine, took him to an empty hallway, and told him to hold onto the gun until after school. Sure enough, in my English class next period, I heard a knock on the door. One of the administrators stuck their head in and said, "Mr. Fernandes, can you step outside please." I got out to the hallway, and right away, they searched me. When they couldn't find the gun, we all went to my locker, and they searched it, too. Still no gun, so they asked all these questions, "Where is it? We know you brought a gun to school. What happened to it?"

They kept asking, and I kept pretending not to know what they were talking about, until they finally said, "Look, so-and-so saw you with a gun at the bus stop. If you don't want to be expelled, you need to tell us where it is." If I wasn't a great gangster, I was a great liar. I told them, off the top of my head, the best lie I've ever come up with. I fessed up to the original plan, then said that, on the bus, I'd had a change of heart. I decided to do the right thing and chucked the gun out of the window of the bus. They, of course, asked where I threw the gun out. I quickly pictured my bus route, and I knew that there was an elementary school we drove past on Ash Street and that the area had a lot of student foot traffic in the morning.

I told them I pitched it on Ash, and they put me in cuffs, and we all drove to the area of Ash where I knew lots of kids traveled, to look for the gun. It didn't turn up, which I knew it wouldn't, and when that happened, I told them that some kid or a parent, a teacher or someone must have stopped and grabbed it at some point. They never did find the gun, and they couldn't prove that I ever brought it onto school premises, but because I had confessed to having it at the bus stop, they suspended me for ten days and scheduled an expulsion hearing on the tenth day. For one reason or another, my expulsion hearing kept getting delayed and they kept extending my suspension until I had missed so much of the year that they gave me an option: repeat the tenth grade or leave the school. I chose to repeat.

All of this is to say that I performed my fair share of antics in high school, both inside the classroom and out. And, except for some bumps of varying size in the road, I didn't face too severe of consequences. Until the first day of my senior year.

I walked into the chorus room, and Ms. Knight, the choral director, told me that Vinny Macrina, the Music Department head, wanted to see me in his office. Vinny and I, after four years of high school, still had not become friendly. He hated me the first day of senior year just as much as he did the first week of my freshman year, which we will discuss in more detail later in the book.

I walked into Vinny's office, and what he said next has been tattooed on my brain ever since. There was no "hello," there was no "how are you," he didn't even nod at me in greeting. He just stood there a look of happy calmness on his face. When I got settled, he looked me dead in my eyes and said, "You are no longer able to be part of the music program here at Brockton High School."

Life paused for a moment. The only thing I could say was, "What?"

"While you are an extremely talented young man, your conduct has given us no choice but to remove you from everything Arts related," said Vinny. I honestly don't remember what happened after that. All I know is, once again, I was in a situation where I felt I had no control.

To this day, I still don't quite know what "conduct" got me kicked out of the music program. I knew I was a royal pain, but I never saw it coming, and there's nothing that happened in the summer between junior and senior year that could have triggered this change. There I was, in my senior year of high school, and the one thing I was good at, the only thing I really cared about, disappeared from my life. Everyone around me was talking about college and scholarships, and I had been forced from the one glowing spot of my academic history in disgrace. I kept asking myself: did I just throw my future away by acting like an idiot?

I was mad at everyone. Ms. Knight, the school choral director, who felt like my second mom, couldn't do anything to save me. I wanted her to fight for me; I wanted her to do something, but it felt like she totally abandoned me. It didn't feel right—I was Mrs. Fernandes's son. Ms. Knight knew my mother, and Vinny occasionally played at my church with his brass quartet, and I felt like they should have treated me like family, but still, they threw me to the curb. None of my pleading to try to stay in the music program worked. Did I try hard enough? I've asked myself that question for years. Either way, I was out. I lost my very last breath; there was no more wind in my sails. Music had left my world.

Once kicked out of the music program, I went straight into rogue mode. I felt what real anger was, and there was no stopping me. I shut out my chorus friends, teachers, and anyone even remotely related to the music program, as easily as turning off a light switch. On the day Vinny booted me from the program, I went to Vinny's car after school and sliced all four of his tires. There were no cameras or social media sites. I knew I couldn't get caught. If I got accused, I knew no one could prove a damn thing. Of course, the next day, the administration called me into the office and questioned me. Smirking, I denied everything. Everybody knew I did it, but with no proof, what could they possibly do?

Since I was no longer in the music program, what was I going to do with my time? Definitely not schoolwork. This situation just gave me more time to hang out with friends who always had time to hang out. I passed the hours at the Boys and Girls Club, the YMCA, and the east-side projects. I was hanging on Temple Street, Exchange Street, Tremont, Southfield Gardens, and Chatham West. I drank more alcohol, smoked even more weed, and I started to feel firsthand how exciting the streets were. If I'd flirted with being a gangster before, by now I was in love with the idea. Balls deep in the idea.

My parents saw the change I went through, and for a little while, they tried to stop it. They didn't have any real control. I was very independent and wasn't afraid of much. In this period, and through most of high school, my dad and I fought a lot. Well, he swung, I ducked. I never fought back. That year, for the third time since I began high school, he threw me out of the house. Instead of crashing with friends until I could come back, I just went and got an apartment. I remember having to wake myself up, drive my roommate to his job, and then drive myself to high school. At that point, I was living like an independent adult with a job (I worked in food service since age fifteen), a place, and a car. I didn't feel like anyone could tell me shit.

While I was heavily running the streets, I still never crossed "that line." I wasn't selling drugs, doing any hard drugs, committing grand larceny, really "gangbanging" or anything like that. That being said, it is something of a miracle that I survived Brockton High, especially my senior year. I got into a lot of fights, both one-on-one deals and drunken bar brawls. I drove drunk all the time, and got stabbed two more times. When I walked at graduation, the most surprising thing was that I was physically capable of walking.

I wasn't interested in college, but my mother pushed me to apply. My grades weren't great in high school, not because the work was too hard, but simply because I wasn't interested in doing it. Nevertheless, I ended up getting into Bridgewater State College. But there were still three months of summer vacation to get through.

Now that high school was over, I had even more time to sink into my rough life. Looking back, I can see that the summer was a bridge between my high school years and the major arrest that would come about a year later. As my sister once told me, "You strived to be at the bottom of the barrel; you thrived at the bottom of the barrel," and sadly, the following summer, I made her right.

This particular summer, I picked up a couple more petty charges. I never had a gun of my own, but I had friends with guns, and we would head out to the woods and shoot bottles every once in a while. I knew people who shot people; I knew people who had been shot.

Since my senior year of high school, I was a fighter and never needed guns. I was small, but I packed a powerful punch and I was fast. I fought mostly big dudes because little guys seemed like easy targets, but that's not always the case now is it? I liked to fight. It was an adrenaline rush, and I was good at it. So the more I fought, the more confident I got. The more confident I got, the more of an asshole I became.

My first attempt at college did nothing to improve my behavior. Even though I was only fifteen minutes away from home and had already lived on my own a few times, I felt a new level of freedom in college. With that freedom, I wasted my entire first year, partying hard, showing up to class drunk or hungover, or not going at all. I found new and creative ways to ramp up the stupid shit I did when I was drunk. I remember taking a friend's car one night, wasted drunk, to a house where I thought there was a house party. The house seemed dead, but I went in anyway. No one was there. So I took their forty-six-inch TV, put it in my friend's car, and drove back to my dorm.

Whatever dumb shit I got up to in my first year of college was nothing compared to what I did in the summer of '97. I stumbled, drunk and high, across the finish line of my first year on academic probation. I got back to Brockton and, for some reason, started to kick back with three guys who had just been acquaintances of mine in high school: Money, Anthony, and Drizzy. Money was this small Cape Verdean guy who happened to look just like me. We used to play basketball together in high school. Anthony was another Cape Verdean kid, who looked like he was thirty and Spanish, with fair skin. He was one of six kids—all of the others were girls, and he was known for spending a lot of time by himself.

Drizzy was one of the biggest, blackest guys in all of Brockton, and scary as hell. He was known for whooping ass. I always felt safer when Drizzy was around. Out of my whole crew, Drizzy was the one person who really had struggled his entire life. His parents were drug addicts and had been since he was born. They raised him in the worst neighborhoods. He'd never had nice clothes, never had a fresh haircut, and he sold drugs way before anyone else did. The thing is, he tried to make himself better—he played football, tried hard to do good. But it didn't work—he was from the crackhead neighborhood, and the hood didn't let him escape. By the time I finished my first year of college, he, Money, and Anthony were selling crack and cocaine. Like me, Drizzy kept getting pulled deeper into the world of crime. The only difference was that while he had tried to run away from it, I had run straight toward it.

That's probably part of why, when I started selling crack with Drizzy and the gang, they asked me what the hell I was doing. They knew that I didn't come from this world—they knew that my parents had always been able to provide whatever I needed for me. And really, I didn't have a good answer for them. Even then, I still wanted to be a music teacher. During those talks with myself at night, when I saw a performance or heard a choir, I knew that's what I was destined to do, even if I did nothing to pursue that dream. Even though I didn't have an answer for them or myself, I began hanging with Money, Anthony, and Drizzy every day. Money had an older sister who had an apartment on Bartlett Street, Brockton's own drug bazaar. As long as we gave her some money for food, she let us sell whatever we wanted from her porch. It was the perfect situation.

The first couple of times, I just went there to chat, smoke some weed, and drink with my friends. That didn't last long. I started buying 8 balls of crack to sell. I learned how to turn cocaine into crack, how to cut the drugs with baking soda to maximize profit. All the while, I was living with my parents. I would wake up to Ray Charles on the stereo and the sound of the vacuum cleaner running over the living room carpet. My mother had summers off, and many mornings, I would go upstairs, have a great breakfast with Mom, talk to her, laugh with her, then kiss her goodbye, and drive off to sell crack all day from a porch. Even after high school, I continued to live a double life—neither of my parents had any idea what I was doing.

Selling crack isn't all it's cracked up to be. It was a dangerous hustle—not because people would try to rip us off or had guns or anything, but just because addicts could get unpredictable. One time I broke my ankle playing basketball and went around with a cast and crutches. Showing more dedication to this job than any academic pursuit, except for music, I found myself sitting on the porch waiting for crackheads. One time when a truck pulled up, I left my crutches on the porch steps and hobbled my ass over to the pickup. Two white dudes sat in the cab. They said they wanted two twenties, so, stupidly, I put my hand inside the window. I had maybe five in my hand for them to choose from. The passenger reached inside my palm to grab a few, then the driver hit the gas. They dragged me, cast, broken ankle and all, for about ten feet. I could've been killed.

When I managed to get back to the porch, my friends laughed and called me every stupid name in the book. They thought I was an idiot for being so committed to selling something that I really didn't need to be selling. Looking back on it, I guess I wanted them to believe I could do this. I needed someone to say I was good at something. Since leaving the chorus group in high school, I hadn't felt like I belonged, truly, in a group. I still hadn't felt like I was really good at anything. And, these guys out on the porch every day, drinking and smoking (weed— never, ever crack) were a group.

One night, we were at Drizzy's house instead of on the porch, to celebrate his birthday. At the time, he lived in a very, very small one-bedroom apartment in a well-known crack house with maybe twenty apartments. The four of us played cards, smoked, drank, and just had a good time. I got thirsty and wanted something to drink other than beer or water. When I opened Drizzy's fridge, unsurprisingly, I found it empty.

I did not have a car at that time—having wrecked my first car in high school, and dumped the two I'd bought after that—so I told everyone I'd be right back, and I jumped on my bike. It was about 2:00 a.m., and I was absolutely wasted. As I pulled up to the store on my bike, a car pulled up next to me, and the people inside asked if I had any crack. It was an older-looking white man and a white lady about the same age, which, while not being the most common consumers of crack, wasn't unheard of. Without even thinking, I said yeah and gave them what they wanted. They drove off, and I went into the store to grab my drink.

As I walked to the front to pay, I looked out the glass doors and saw tons of police cars pull up to a screeching halt. I sobered up real quick, just for a moment, and took the remaining drugs and stashed them in a candy box on a shelf. When the police rushed into the store, they immediately grabbed me and began going through my pockets. I acted exactly as I acted when I got searched for the gun in high school—while they kept yelling, "Where is it, where is it?" I just acted like I had no idea what the fuck they were doing. After they found nothing on me, they completely ransacked the store. The poor cashier at the counter kept yelling at them to stop, but of course, they didn't listen. They went through every box and every shelf around me, and when they unearthed my stash, they cuffed me and escorted me outside. The same car that I had served minutes before drove by, looked me over, gave a little nod, and into the back of the cruiser I went. Later, I would learn that the two people I served in the car were undercover state troopers. I had graduated from misdemeanors to felonies. I was officially a criminal.

Whatever sobriety I gained when the cop cars came tearing into the lot fled from me when I got into the back of the cruiser. I was too hammered to see straight and too hammered to process what was happening to me. I don't remember the ride over at all—just getting to the Brockton police station's holding cell. At the back of my mind, a voice was shouting through the alcohol fog that my life was about to change. Seeing the cops around me confirmed that—they all looked at me like I was some sort of poor dumbass. One guy dropped by and handed me a pamphlet that said, "Jesus Saves" on the front.

That night, they gave me a phone call. I was drunk, but I wasn't drunk enough to call my parents. I called my friends instead, but when they found out my bail was five thousand dollars, I was on my own. Shortly after that, I passed out on the bench in the holding cell. When I woke up, I had a killer hangover, and that's when I realized just how much trouble I was in. They offered me another phone call, but there was no way I was going to call my parents. I figured they'd hold me for about three days, then release me on my own recognizance, and I'd just go home like nothing happened. My parents probably wouldn't worry—it wasn't the first time I didn't come back for days, and I, on some level, thought I could just pretend nothing had happened.

Imagine my surprise when, that very morning, an officer came into the holding cell and told me my father had just bailed me out. I didn't move for a solid ten seconds, and I seriously considered asking if I could just stay in the holding cell. I would later learn that a friend of mine who worked as a police dispatcher had heard my name and called my parents. It was the longest walk ever from the cell to the release area. My dad was a screamer, and he sometimes threw punches, and I didn't know what to expect. Instead of yelling, the ride home from the police station was silent. When we got home, his first question to me was, "Are you doing drugs or are you selling drugs?" I knew that he was aware I smoked weed, but the way he said it, he believed I was an addict myself. I told him hell no I wasn't doing crack, I was just selling it. All I really remember from the rest of that conversation was hearing him say, "You're gonna pay for that. You want to be out there runnin' around like these fucking knuckleheads, you're about to see what happens to knuckleheads."

My mom hired a lawyer for me. A court-appointed lawyer was pretty much a death sentence in Brockton, and my mother knew this. Even after I had messed up, in a big way, she gave me everything she could. Again, I can only imagine the pain my mother felt, the helplessness of realizing that I had become something that she never envisioned. I had become everything she tried to keep away from me. From the private school in fifth grade to Latin school, from the lessons she taught me to my values and morals—everything positive that this amazing woman ingrained in me, I took for granted, ignored, fought against, and rejected, just to become the world's worst drug dealer.

2

FROM FREEDOM TO
ROCK AND ROLL

"Happiness is synthetic—you either create it, or you don't.
Happiness that lasts is earned through your habits."
~ Jack Shepherd, better known to me as Gpop

Getting out of jail was just as scary as going in. I had been incarcerated for almost a year before I was released, and in that time, amazingly, I had gotten used to the structure of jail. The week leading up to my release was agonizing. *What would I do when I got out? How would people look at me? How would my mom, my girlfriend, and strangers treat me?*

I woke up on the morning of my release with my stomach in knots at the Massachusetts State Boot Camp. I took some time that morning to reflect on my journey. Over the last year, I had survived the Plymouth County

Correctional Facility and the state run correctional boot camp, which was still jail, only with better food, a lot more exercising and a ton of yelling. I had barely eaten, barely slept. It wasn't just nerves: I was also excited, of course. It felt like every childhood Christmas combined. Yet nothing felt real, and nothing seemed right. That day was the first time I'd put on a pair of jeans in a year, and they felt strange. I had gotten so used to polyester khakis that I felt nearly indecent.

When they finally called for me, I was in a daze. I was dressed in my street clothes, but I was still shining my prison-issued shoes, just to pass the time. I knew I was leaving soon and I would never wear them again, but I had to do something. I remember looking out a window as they called my name over the speaker, thinking about how a year earlier, I had been looking out the same window thinking I couldn't imagine being free. It was a great window. It pointed toward the entrance to the boot camp. This was where all of the DIs parked, and I was able to see everyone coming and going. Although it was just a small, two-foot-by-two-foot window, it was like looking out into the free world. It was my connection to normal life, to normalcy. During shift changes, I would see the DIs taking off their boot camp gear, instantly morphing back into regular people, and getting in their cars. At times, how I longed to be able to just walk out with them. Now that I was free, it was almost reversed. I felt apprehensive about leaving.

They brought me to a waiting room, where a TV played reruns of *The Three Stooges.* How appropriate. I hated that show my entire life on a normal day, but this wasn't a normal day. Watching these idiots fumble around with their stupidness was just what I needed. I was going home, and I could not have cared less about what was on that TV. I hadn't watched TV for eight months, so just about anything seemed good at that point.

I couldn't focus on it anyway, because at that moment, in the waiting room, I started to realize how changed I'd felt by jail. Would I spend the rest of my life dodging confrontation, sitting through endless episodes of *The Three Stooges*, because I thought some faceless entity still could control my future? Another person was in the waiting room with me, and I don't know what they were thinking about, we didn't talk much, but I'm sure our thoughts were similar.

We sat in silence for about an hour, and then a CO and a lieutenant fetched me for processing. When I left the waiting room, they didn't walk me through the prisoners' door, but instead through the staff door. I was on my way back to becoming a civilian. They asked me for my social security number, release address, etc., to help verify who I was. I immediately noticed that the COs treated me totally differently than before. They didn't talk down to me, swear to me, avoid my eyes, or yell. They smiled, joked around. They were friendly and genuinely happy for me.

I went through an electronic bar gate, and there was a guy behind glass. This was "control," where they made all the PA announcements. I had never seen it before. He asked me more questions again for verification, and then I was taken to another waiting room and told to have a seat. I could see beyond the glass doors that led to the outside. No fence. No nothing. Freedom.

Then, I heard the staff say that the person who was there to pick me up, Ana, my high school sweetheart and the woman would later become the mother of my children, was outside already. I nodded but stayed sitting. Then, one of the COs looked at me and said, "You can go ..."

I said out loud, "Oh!"

The COs laughed at me. I just wasn't used to it—a couple of hours earlier, and that would have been an escape attempt. They would have chased me, tased me, clubbed me. But now, I stood up and walked out into the bright sun, where Ana waited for me. I hugged her, gave her a kiss, and got in the car. We started driving. It was quiet for the first few miles, except for when one of us would marvel at the fact that I was finally here, finally free. I could tell that Ana didn't quite know how to act around me, even though we'd seen each other at every visit. It was a lot different. And I didn't know how to act, either. I'd spent months never getting close to a car, to the road, and now here I was with all these trees and little gray buildings sliding by.

The first post-prison meal I wanted was a really good burger, so we stopped at Friendly's. It was right between breakfast and lunch, so we could order from either menu. I just told them to give me something with bacon, and they did. And I was happy. But they got Ana's order wrong and she got upset about it, to the point that she had an argument with an employee.

Now, this is not who Ana usually was. She understands that a Friendly's employee has it hard enough without having to be friendly to some ticked-off customer. But she was already in a weird mood, because so much of that day had been strange, and, somehow, not as happy as either of us had hoped. So she exploded, and during the entire argument with the employee, I felt sweat explode across my body, my hairs stood on end. My body thought I was still in jail, where any sign of confrontation meant that something bad can, and will, go down.

When we finished eating, we left the restaurant and went to my parents' house. Since I had nowhere else to go, I would be staying with them until I got back on my feet. I went inside, and the air felt weird. As strange as it sounds, my parents' house felt cramped.

When you are locked up, the cells are super small, and you spend most of your time in a HUGE open space. A day room of sorts, but with about two hundred other inmates. On top of that, it was silent. In jail, the noise is constant: a PA announcement, the inmates chatting, the clattering of materials, a guard pacing. In all that silence, I felt alone with my thoughts and doubts. I tried to watch TV in the living room, but being able to watch whatever I want with a remote control in my hand was too weird. So, I went back to my room, sat on the floor, and cried.

Here I was, free, and I felt more trapped than ever. It took me forever to fall asleep that night. I did eventually, and when I woke up, I was so nervous that I shook, and I couldn't figure out where I was at first. Eventually, I realized I was in my parents' house. Then my first thought was: "Yep, still alone."

I'd had a lot of time in jail to evaluate myself and to plan for my future. I knew I wanted to do bigger and better things, but it would be easier said than done. There had to be a change. My days of attempting to sell drugs were over, and I needed to find a way to make some money. Deep down in my heart, I knew that music was still the foundation of my soul and that I wanted to teach. But I didn't have the courage to jump right back into music, and having just been released from jail, I didn't have the confidence to walk into a school or any place that dealt with children and ask for a job. On top of that, I hadn't played an instrument in years, but I felt pressure to move because everyone was waiting for me to do something.

My first step was staying away from the things that put me in jail in the first place. I had no intention of contacting any of the friends I was hanging out with prior, but I knew that I would bump into them on the street at some point. I had to be strong and keep my mind focused, as I knew that hanging around those friends could torpedo my forward progress, for two reasons: the first was that many of them were still selling drugs, and that was not a lifestyle I wanted to revisit. Additionally, I'd learned that hanging around negative people can pull you down. And these were some negative dudes.

They were the kinds of people who would complain about their problems and blame any sort of issue on something external. And this, I started to realize while in jail, is dangerous. It can make you start to focus more on the problems and less on the solutions.

I had gone down that path while I was in jail, constantly blaming people, making excuses for myself, claiming that I had been wronged. But none of that helped anything, and in the end, it just made me more depressed, because it put me in the mindset of seeing myself as a victim of fate, instead of someone who could control my own circumstances.

That being said, right after my release, I experienced an extreme sense of negativity. Life hadn't gone the way I wanted it to, but when it came down to it, I had to acknowledge that I had the same twenty-four hours in the day as everyone else. I noted that happy people make their time count. Instead of complaining about how things could have been or should have been, they reflect on everything they have to be grateful for. Then they find the best solution available to the problem, tackle it, and move on. Nothing fuels unhappiness like pessimism. The problem with a pessimistic attitude is that it becomes a self-fulfilling prophecy: if you expect bad things, you're more likely to get bad things. Pessimistic thoughts are hard to shake off until you recognize how illogical they are. When I forced myself to look at the facts, I saw that things were not nearly as bad as they seemed. But I was still scared.

Like fear, the past and the future are products of our minds. No amount of guilt could undo my past, and no amount of anxiety could improve my future. I knew this, and I did my best to focus on living in the present moment. It would be impossible for me to reach my full potential if I was constantly unable to fully embrace my reality. To live in the present moment, I had to accept my past and accept the uncertainty of my future. If I didn't make peace with my past, it was never going to leave me, and it would create my future. I also didn't want to place unnecessary expectations on myself. Worry has no place in the here and now. As Mark Twain said, "Worrying is like paying a debt you don't owe."

Practicing being present was a process, and one that I'm still working on. But in the short term, it helped. Not long after being released, I got a job working for Rent-A-Center as a furniture delivery guy. It wasn't my dream job to deliver furniture, but I needed a full-time job with benefits to prove that I was ready to integrate myself back into society in a positive way. Like most things in my life, I didn't settle for what I was given. I worked my ass off and managed to wiggle my way right to the top of the food chain at Rent-A-Center. I first got promoted to Accounts Manager and then moved straight up the ladder to Assistant Manager, and got very close to running my own store.

My rise was so rapid because my higher-ups saw my hustle. Pete was the first manager I worked for. He was an older white gentleman in his upper sixties, very rough around the edges, but with a soft filling. Most people feared him and kept their distance; I, on the other hand, did not. Pete and I became close friends, and he admired my work ethic. I was a little guy with spunk. I prided myself on being the smallest member of the team that also worked the hardest. I was a great salesman, I could deliver furniture, I could repair furniture, I could run the books, I learned the computer systems, and I did it all. Pete took me under his wing and showed me the way, and he fought for me to get those promotions.

I did exactly what everybody wanted me to do. I found a job, I got an apartment, I had a car, and I was working full-time. I should've been content, right? Wrong. My days became so repetitive: wake up, go to work, and come home from work just to get ready for work again. I was not doing anything that was feeding my soul or making me happy. I wasn't doing anything that gave me a real sense of accomplishment when I came home. My mother always had told me to find something I was good at, and then find a way to make money from it. My problem was that I was always good at making money, but I'd never had a job that gave me what I really needed.

I knew something needed to change; I just didn't know what. I'll never forget the day. It was a Tuesday. I was sitting on my couch watching TV, and it hit me in the head like a bag of bricks. I needed out. I needed to get away from everything I knew. I needed a fresh start. I needed to go to a place where I didn't have this history, where people wouldn't know who I was or what I had done, where there weren't temptations to fall into old patterns. It was the only way that I truly ever was going to see if I had what it takes to make it. So I had to figure out a plan to get out of Massachusetts. Who did I know? Who would let me come stay with them with no money, no job, no nothing? And more important than that, what was I going to do?

I'd always known that I needed music in my life, but I had gone so long without it that I was anxious to dive back into the music world. Still, I knew that if I really wanted to move forward, to find a fulfilling life, I would have to rely on music. So I asked myself, *where could I go where I could bring music back into my life?* Once I did that, I knew what I had to do. My uncle Jeff, my mom's brother, lived very close to West Palm Beach. He and my aunt Linda had been singing together since I was a child. They'd done the cruise ship thing, they'd done the casino thing, they had sung at more nightclubs than most people have ever thought of being in. It was a no-brainer.

That night, I called my uncle and asked him if it would be all right if I came down to Florida to stay with them for a while. I explained to him that I had found nothing but trouble in Brockton, and I needed a change of scenery in order to better my life. He thought it was a wonderful idea, but he had to check with his wife first, and he would give me a call back. I was excited.

The next day, a Wednesday, Uncle Jeff called me back and told me that he and his wife had decided that they would open their home to me and let me stay. I couldn't believe it! I knew I had to act fast before I changed my mind. I loaded up my car, and I was out.

I drove to Port St. Lucie, Florida, by myself, twenty-three hours straight. The ride down seemed like an eternity, and I loved it. Each state I drove through, it was as if, in my mind, I was crossing that state out of my life, much like I'd crossed off the days while waiting to be released from jail. With every mile, I was farther and farther away from who I didn't want to be and closer to who I wanted to become. I was literally driving to the Promised Land.

When I moved to Florida, I had nothing but my car and a few hundred bucks. I had no idea what I was going to do when I got there. I knew I had to find a job immediately, just to bring in a little bit of money to contribute to my aunt and uncle, who had so graciously opened their home to me.

I didn't know anyone besides my family. On maybe my third day there, I met Rich. I had gone to a local bar that was right down the street from my aunt and my uncle's house. I remember clearly because I saw the sign earlier that day that read "Ladies Night Tonight." If you're ever a bachelor in a new town, and you see a sign that says "Ladies Night Tonight," that's where you want to be, or at least that's where I wanted to be.

That night, I was sitting at the bar, and across from me, I saw a black gentleman sitting by himself. He looked about my age, was freshly dressed, and didn't look too intimidating. After everything I'd been through, I had nothing to lose. So I walked up to this guy and said, "Hey, I'm new here, just moved to town and I don't know anybody. I saw you were sitting here by yourself, and I said, 'What the hell, I might as well introduce myself and make a new friend.' What's poppin?"

And that's exactly what happened. Rich and I became best friends, but not before he said, "What's poppin? You gotta be from up North."

Ironically, Rich and I were the same age and had the same dominant personality, but he was what I wished I was, except his father had been a drug dealer, and he had every reason to sell drugs. Rich had been a total knucklehead like me in high school, but had managed to straighten out his life right after graduating. He joined the Army right out of high school, and it made him a man. It was his way out, and he took advantage of the opportunity. He'd already known he didn't want to be a thug. He'd become one because it was all he knew, but he wanted more. The military had saved him and it was his choice to join. Maybe this was fate, maybe it was luck, maybe it was destiny. Whatever it was, I was happy that I had met someone so positive and uplifting.

In addition to being an amazing human being, he also became exactly the connection I needed to find work. Rich had recently purchased his first truck, a big tractor-trailer, and he was a private contractor for Rooms To Go, a major furniture distributor. He was always looking for good guys to join him on his daily routes. He delivered furniture up and down the East Coast of Florida and paid cash. He had me at "cash."

Working for Rich became my first source of income as a Floridian. However, it wasn't music, and I'd gone down there to work in music. Still, I had to start somewhere. I started working with him almost immediately. So during the day, I was with Rich, and at night, my aunt and uncle were steadily performing three or four times a week. I went to every single one of their shows, and at every show, they would call me to the stage to sing a few tunes just to get me back into the swing.

I'll never forget a night in Palm Beach at the New York Bar and Grill. My aunt and uncle called me up onstage to sing *Ain't Too Proud To Beg* by The Temptations. As usual, when I got on the mic, I introduced myself as Jeff and

Linda's nephew from Boston. Every time I got onstage, I made it a point to let everybody know that I just moved to Florida, and I was so happy to be there back in the music biz with my family. This particular night, there were two gentlemen sitting at a table with their wives.

They watched me like hawks eyeing a mouse. They whispered to each other every once in a while as they continued to watch me for the entire night. When I got offstage, they walked over to me, very mob-like, and the little bald one, Sal, informed me that they were part of a Fifties and Sixties doo-wop group that was looking for one more member.

"What do you know about doo-wop?" Sal asked.

I chuckled and responded, "I probably know just as much as you."

What he didn't know is that although my dad was not musical in any way, shape, or form, he loved listening to music. I grew up listening to oldies 103.3 in Boston every single day. I knew all there was to know about doo-wop, inside and out. I knew the oldies like I knew English. It was a match made in Motown. A week later, I was the fourth and final member of Sha-Boom.

A few short months later, we were asked to open a show for the Temptations in Fort Pierce, Florida, in front of three thousand people. During the show, I looked to the side of the stage and saw The Temptations watching me sing. It was definitely one of the top moments I've experienced.

As awesome as all this was, with music being back in my life, the one area where I was still unsatisfied was in my desire to teach. Until one night, a woman who was at one of our performances approached me. She worked for the county and asked me if there was any way I could get kids to do what we were doing. It felt like divine intervention, like God had dropped this woman out of the sky. This was where I truly hit my stride. The trifecta was complete. She ended up getting me a job with the Boys and Girls Club, run by the county, and there I started a music program that consisted of singing and dancing.

When I say I was working in the hood, I was working in the HOOD! But this was not a hood I was used to. This was poverty at a level that I had never experienced before. This was down South poverty. These kids didn't have food to eat when they went home at night. These kids had skin rashes and malnourished bodies. It was like nothing I'd ever seen before. I'm not saying that these extremes did not exist back home, but even the poorest people I knew and associated with did not live like this. It was sad and eye-opening for me. These kids needed help, and I was going to do all I could for them. My first day there, they looked at me in awe, the kids and the staff. I was "red boned" and somewhat educated. To them, I might as well have been DJ Khaled; I was a fucking hit and anything I did was FULLY supported. I felt respected and valued. Beyond what I could do for them, it was exactly what I needed for myself, too.

Maybe it was destiny, maybe it was pure luck, maybe I was being rewarded for making the life-changing move to the other side of the country. Either way, I was on my way. Music had finally made its way back into my life, and I had received the opportunity to work with kids and help to bring more music into their lives.

It seemed like a miracle. All of a sudden, here I was, a guy who'd decided to drive to Florida with nothing, and now I had a day job that paid cash, I was singing in a Fifties and Sixties doo-wop group at night, which happened to be my favorite music, and I was teaching kids, all within my first year.

I spent a good five years living in Florida, until September 7, 2004, when Hurricane Frances hit. All of my belongings were destroyed in the hurricane. I had no money saved. While I had accumulated some things during my stay in Florida, I did not have renters insurance, so when the roof of the apartment building began to come apart during the hurricane, I ran to a neighbor's house and watched all of my stuff get destroyed. While the owner of the house got a healthy insurance check, I was stuck with a handshake and many, "I'm so sorry for your loss" conversations.

My uncle and aunt's house was hit hard as well, so I couldn't find it in myself to ask them to let me stay there again when they were struggling just to put the pieces of their lives back together. This was a stressful time for me, and I gave in to the pressure. I gave up everything I'd worked so hard for and moved back to the Brockton Box, like most who move out do. It was a blow to my soul and my confidence.

The first day I woke up and realized that I was back in Brockton was excruciating. The weather difference alone was enough to drive a man mad. I questioned for a long time if I had made the right decision, and today, as I write this, I can say that I did. But even then, I tried to stay positive, and, once again, I was forced to believe that positivity would bring positive results.

I stayed away from old friends, as I had no desire to hang on the corner, wasting my life away again. I was much more focused. While music was still at the forefront of my brain, once again I needed to find a way to make money. With my experience, I quickly got a job at the YMCA, teaching music in the same capacity I'd taught in Florida at the Boys and Girls Club. But it wasn't enough to pay the rent.

By my third month back in Massachusetts, my mother noticed that I was getting agitated. That motherly instinct is so real. Once again, she saw I was at a crossroads where I could potentially take another wrong turn. I can only imagine what she felt at that time. What I do know is that she was not going to let me fall again, and she took action.

I was completely oblivious to her plan until after she had already set things in motion, and she asked me, "Do you remember Lou Siagel?"

I replied, "Of course I do!" Lou Siagel was my mother's colleague at Boston Latin school. He was a man I loved, respected, and owed a great deal to for all that he had contributed to my life. She continued, "I think he has a son who's doing something with music." I found out later that she already knew the whole time that he was a super successful musician, entertainer, and entrepreneur that I needed to meet.

She said that she had already talked to Lou and they both thought that Steve (Lou's son) and I should meet. So, I was given his phone number and he was given mine. Steve and I played phone tag for about three weeks. I can honestly say that I was ready to give up, and I said to my mother, "Mama, I've called this guy ten times, and I still haven't heard back. I give up!"

My mother spoke with force and said, "You WILL keep calling him until you get ahold of him!" Little did I know my mother had reached out to Lou again, and once Lou heard that Steve had not reached out to me, he must've been stern with his son as well, because Steve called me a couple of days later and we set a time to meet at his office.

When I met with Steve for the first time, I was introduced to a world that was the polar opposite of the poverty I witnessed at the Boys and Girls Club where I'd worked in Florida. Little did I know that Steve Siagel was the bar mitzvah king of New England. I had never been to a bar mitzvah and, honestly, didn't even know what a bar mitzvah was, but I soon found out.

After learning about my experience in Florida with the kids, my experience with Sha-Boom on the microphone, and my love of dance, Steve thought it would be a good idea to give me a shot. He asked me what I was doing that very night, to which I responded, "Nothing." He told me to wear all black and meet me at the address he wrote down on a piece of paper. I had no idea what I was getting myself into. He just told me that I was going to be a party motivator and would have someone there to train me.

When I arrived at this venue, I couldn't believe my eyes. And when I found out it was a party for a thirteen-year-old kid, I was astonished. I had never been around people with so much money, or such elegance. The contrast between the poverty I'd seen in Florida just a few months before, was drastic. For most Americans up North, poverty means families in run-down housing in large cities where the industry has moved away. The true depth of racial poverty, however, is found in rural areas of the South, where living conditions are even more run-down and industry never really started up.

Since I was sent there to be a party motivator, my job was easy. All I did was to mingle with the kids on the dance floor while I watched Steve, who was the Emcee for the night, play lots of games, lead the Jewish blessings over the bread and wine, and pretty much run the party. I specifically remember a white guy who was also there training as an Emcee. As I write this, I've been with the company for almost twenty years now, so it's safe to say that I've seen lots of Emcee's come and go, and I can honestly say that guy was awful.

And then it happened. At one point in the party when everybody was rocking out on the dance floor, Steve looked at me and said, "Do you want to take the mic for a second?" I gave him the Jean-Claude Van Damme hands like in Bloodsport, that basically said "Bring It On!" And my career with Siagel Productions began. It's a career and a friendship that is still going strong today. Side note: that white guy who was training to be an Emcee—I never saw him again.

So now, I was making great money at Siagel, surrounded by inspirational people, and enjoying life. But I still wasn't satisfied. Music was back in my life, but not how it was supposed to be. I wasn't ready to settle, but I couldn't find the motivation to get past my boundaries until something drastic happened and turned my life upside down as nothing had done before.

During this time, I was living in the basement of my parents' house, and it was a nice, quiet existence. I know, this doesn't sound like rock bottom. And it wasn't. But it wasn't my high point either—I was floating somewhere between the waves and the rocky ocean floor, not doing any more than I needed to do to avoid sinking. Rock bottom was waiting for me.

3

HITTING ROCK BOTTOM

"Rock bottom became the solid foundation
on which I rebuilt my life."
~ J.K. Rowling

On any given Saturday, I looked forward to waking up, going upstairs, and eating the leftovers from Mom and Dad's early morning breakfast. They were both early birds and woke up between 4:00 and 5:00 a.m., even on days they didn't have to work. As sure as the sun rose each and every day, I knew every Saturday morning, there would be something waiting for me on the stove.

This particular Saturday, I overslept. I had agreed to help a friend who owned a dance academy. Her recital was that day, and I was set to play the music for all the different groups that were going to be onstage performing. I was supposed to be at the recital, which was being held at Brockton High School, at 11:00 a.m. I woke up at about

10:30 a.m. As I rushed to gather my things, I realized I wasn't going to have enough time to run upstairs and grab a bite. I darted out the door. I remember seeing my mom's car in the driveway, but my dad's truck was gone. Most Saturdays after their morning breakfast, my mom would begin her chores or hit the road and start running errands. My dad would either start landscaping the yard, as he loved to do, or he'd be at work collecting the overtime that he bragged so much about. When I saw her car, I automatically assumed that she was either in the middle of her chores, in her room watching TV, or doing something upstairs.

When I arrived at the high school, I began setting up my equipment and getting ready for the recital. After I finished, my phone rang. It was my dad. I thought, *He knows I'm at work, so I'll just give him a call when I'm done*, and I let it go to voicemail. Within seconds, he called back, and once again I sent him to voicemail. When he called back the third time, I knew something was wrong, so I answered the phone. My dad sounded like I'd never heard him before.

He simply said something was wrong with my mother, and that I should get to Brockton Hospital as quickly as possible. I could hear the severity of the situation in the tone of his voice. I knew something awful had happened.

Without a moment's hesitation, I ran out of the auditorium. To this day, I have no idea who played the music for that recital, I have no idea who packed up my equipment, and I also have no idea who returned my sound equipment to my dad's house. All I know is that I ran out of that place as fast as I could and drove as fast as I could to Brockton Hospital.

When I arrived at the hospital, it was an eerie, familiar feeling. My best friend, Marc Jean, had passed away in that same hospital just four years prior from bacterial meningitis. His death was so unexpected and sudden. He died just twenty-four hours after feeling sick.

When I found my family, I was informed that the medical helicopter had already moved her to Tufts Medical Center in Boston, where she would get the best possible care. From the look on my dad's face, though, I knew this was not going to have the ending we so desperately wanted. Dad kept saying, "She's gone."

When we arrived at Tufts, the doctors told us that she was in a coma. She was basically brain-dead, and although they had performed emergency surgery, right now the only thing keeping her alive was a machine.

They let us go upstairs to see her. When I walked into the room, I completely lost it, yelling, "How could you leave me like this!" Kneeling on both knees, because I couldn't find the strength to stand up, I wept, and I wept hard. I stayed by her bedside, whispering, at first telling her how much I loved her and how sorry I was for the mistakes I'd made, the moments when I had taken her for granted. I stayed for about an hour, and I couldn't take it anymore. My father gave the doctors permission to pull the plug when we left, and they did. She was gone. The official cause of death: brain aneurysm.

The whole thing was completely unexpected—she died just three days before her official retirement from teaching, a couple of weeks before her birthday, and a week before a surprise retirement party my sisters and I had planned for her. Two hundred and fifty people were scheduled to attend the party. It ended up being her memorial service.

I had always operated under the assumption that brain aneurysms were unavoidable, bad luck, and came with no warning signs—the way some people just get struck by lightning. Most people believe this. As my family and I processed the death, we spent hours talking about what a surprise it was. But, as we talked, we started to realize that there had been warning signs. She had the WHOL (worst headache of her life) for about two weeks before the aneurysm ruptured, not the typical nagging sinus headache or migraine, but something different.

I found out later that she had mentioned the pain to one of my sisters, and my sister hadn't thought anything of it. Who would? But, in hindsight, after what happened, it seemed huge. Like one of the biggest mistakes any of us had ever made. In moments like these, people always look for things they could have done differently, and ways the tragedy could have been prevented, and they end up blaming themselves. I think all of us did that, to some extent.

Both of my sisters lived out of state at the time, and they returned to their homes a few weeks after the funeral and memorial service. We were all very close, but after that initial period of mourning, each of us retreated into our own bubble of grief. We didn't know what to do without our matriarch there to guide us.

A couple of days after my mother died, I lay in my bathtub soaking, and called her cell phone. She didn't answer, but you knew that already. I heard her voice on the recording. I cried and called back at least five times just to hear that beautiful voice. I missed her.

I can't explain why I rang her old number, any more than I can explain why I had always felt the need to put her in a headlock and kiss the top of her head whenever I saw her, or why I consistently apologized for being so mean to her as a teenager. When she first died, it was heartbreak. It was intense and painful and followed me around with every single breath, dragging behind me like a boulder.

Losing a mother is like being on a sinking ship that is now at the mercy of the deepest ocean. I bobbed around without an anchor to bring me back to the same balanced spot each time, a spot I just couldn't get right. I spent my time sideways, upside down, right-side up, sinking to the ocean floor, and floating back up, being carried on the current to depths of grief where I had never been before.

With my family gone, either physically or emotionally, and having just been laid off, I had a lot of time to fill. I spent it numbing myself.

The term "hitting rock bottom" is usually used when talking about someone with an addiction issue, but it doesn't just describe addiction. It can be used to describe the bottom point of anybody's life, and, in some ways, hitting rock bottom can be a good thing. We can be so focused on our paths that we never raise our heads to look at where we are going—unless something forces us to. When the path we take leads so far down a canyon that there's no light, the only way forward is up. This is exactly what happened to me.

Anyone who knows me knows that the Energizer Bunny has nothing on me. I'm always on the move, full-throttle. But after my mom died, my energy was so diminished, and I had no desire to be out around people or even leave the house. I can say one good thing about my behavior at that time: I didn't do anything really stupid, as most would have expected me to. A few years, hell, even a few months before, if I had faced that same situation, I don't know what I would have done. Probably something dumb and reckless, some way of lashing out that might have landed me back in jail or in the hospital. That Greg Fernandes was gone.

I'd been humbled by the birth of my daughter ten months earlier. Becoming a parent changes everything, and this was one of the best changes that had happened to me. I'd never felt this sort of love or responsibility before, and I took a lot of strength from it. But when my mom died, it brought about a depth and type of pain that I'd never felt before, either.

It wasn't until after my family left and I had all that time on my own that I truly hit rock bottom. It came with the worst feeling of depression. Everything I did carried so much *resistance*, became so *difficult*, took so much *effort*, and every moment of every single day was an absolute nightmare. There were very dark moments when my anger and frustration became unbearable. I felt numb, and for a long time, I couldn't believe that my mother was truly gone. It had been so sudden. I needed a way to cope, and I turned to two old crutches: alcohol and marijuana. This time, though, I also leaned on a third leg: prescription painkillers.

Of course, none of this took the pain away. All it did was rob me of my current moment. For a short time, I had confused this feeling of timelessness, of numbness, with progress. My alcohol use became more and more excessive—I was drinking a full fifth of Hennessy a day. Since alcohol is a depressant, it dragged me down even more. The painkillers did exactly what they said they'd do: kill the pain. But that pain they killed was a true, authentic, and vital part of me. I needed to feel it, needed to have it, and when the pills killed it off, I only felt worse.

On the other hand, being sober was unbearable. I thought that if I could understand "why she died" and "why this happened to my mom," I could accept it more easily and therefore cope with it. I spent all of my time going over these questions, searching for answers that didn't exist. I was drowning, pun intended, in this "why me?" cycle. I was trapped, not making any progress forward. What's crazy is that I was completely functional, despite the hell I was going through on a daily basis. Although I was given time off from work, there was still much to be done. I helped plan the memorial that was supposed to be her retirement party. I was still a parent with a ten-month-old, and since my mother took care of all the bills and the administrative part of my parents' relationship, it was an absolute nightmare dealing with Dad and these issues. I probably could have continued for a while longer, but that was not about to happen. I realized I needed to do something different. I needed to make a big change.

I needed to detox myself and get my mind back to reality. I tried to stop drinking and taking pills on my own, throwing out my stash one night a few weeks after my mom died. It didn't last. That very night, I ran to the liquor store and bought a few pints of beer. I was in too deep. After that night of my failed attempt at cold turkey, I Googled detox centers from my cell phone. I was too ashamed to ask my dad, sisters, or mentors for help. I knew the only way I was going to clean up was to go cold turkey, and I needed to be away from familiar faces. This new, profound pain made me take an action that would have seemed unthinkable just months before. I didn't want it in me and was willing to do anything I could to eradicate it.

I found a detox center in Quincy, Massachusetts, that had an opening. I called and explained my situation, and before the woman had a chance to ask me too many questions, I hung up, jumped in the car, and drove to the facility. Driving to the detox center was a surreal experience. I was happy to be going and proud of myself for making the effort. At the same time, I felt like I was driving myself to jail. The facility was at the end of a long, skinny peninsula that I never even knew existed. The road seemed to go on forever as I kept driving past large, empty stretches of swamp land. There weren't any other buildings on that stretch of peninsula, or so it seemed, and it was nearly an hour's drive from the heart of Quincy. The building I pulled up to looked like an insane asylum—made from stone with bars on every window. It looked like every evil castle Disney had ever created. I almost expected the sky to darken and a black cloud of bats to fly circles around the building at any moment.

After parking and getting out of my car, I hit the buzzer at the door and a voice said, "Can I help you?"

The first thing that came out of my mouth was, "Yes, you can."

I got buzzed in and discovered that the inside matched the outside's imposing tone. The shiny linoleum floors and the khaki-colored walls looked familiar to me, a shitty kind of familiar that reminded me of jail, courthouses, and boot camp. I must have asked myself, "What the hell am I doing here?" ten times as I walked up the echoey stairwell to the main office.

When I got to the desk, a large woman stared me down. She didn't say anything. I just stared back. She obviously wanted me to speak first, and there was an awkward silence for about five seconds as we each tried to outlast the other. She won. I told this intake person my story, about how my mother had died, and I was not in a good place, and that I wanted to check myself into rehab. When she heard that, she responded with a shockingly loud, "What'd you say?"

I then realized that this was not going to be as easy as I'd expected—and that I must have thrown her off her game. She was utterly befuddled, and kept asking me if I had been sent there by a judge, counselor, or some other office. I explained to her over and over again that I personally had driven myself to the detox center, and I wanted to check myself in. I'd like to clean up my life, I explained. Apparently, this didn't happen often, if at all, at this rehab center. For me, I had simply had enough, and I had to do what I had to do to make myself right again. After a long conversation with her and a few other people, they finally admitted me into the detox center.

Several factors determine the length of one's stay at a detox center. This particular place had a one-, two-, three-, and four-week program. One factor is the type of drug use. Since my drug use was minimal, and my biggest problem was drinking, I chose the two-week program. Another factor in choosing a short detox program is your family life. I was not married or with the mother of my daughter, but I was a brand-new parent, and it would have been damn near impossible for me to stay away from my ten-month-old daughter for more than two weeks. I also had a job, which also made it impossible for me to enter a lengthy rehab program. Luckily, my daughter's mother was able to play Mom and Dad while I cleaned myself up, and Steve Siagel made sure that all of my events were covered. My daughter and my job were secure, which made my decision a no-brainer.

I handed in all of my belongings, and this is when the reality of treatment hit hard. The staff brought me to a small room where I was strip-searched. Even though the perimeter of the facility had no fence, and there were no correctional officers, it still felt like jail. The facility kept to a strict schedule. Meals were served at specific times. Groups were held on a regular basis, at specific times. Patients were expected to attend everything. Staff let people slide when people skipped a meeting from time to time, but I came around quicker than most. I wanted to do stuff, get better, and get the hell out of there. So in essence, it really felt like I was back in jail, except this time, I was happy to be there—for the most part.

The first couple of nights were hell, physically and mentally. Physically, my body was reacting to the sudden lack of poison it had grown dependent on. Psychologically,

I was a roller coaster of emotions. While still dealing with my mother's death, being there made me feel a sense of shame, agony, sadness, and embarrassment.

I passed the first night in the small, white and tan dorm room they gave me. The nursing staff kept coming in through the night, attempting to give me medications to aid with my detox. I kept rejecting them, as this seemed counterproductive. Didn't I come here to STOP taking pills? Now you want me to take pills to stop taking pills? They were always surprised by my refusals. I guess to them it was like someone refusing Novocain at the dentist.

COLD TURKEY

It's true what they say—the first three nights of going cold turkey are the hardest. They passed in a blur of physical and psychological pain, and after that, I was able to take stock of my situation and surroundings. Although I considered myself to be in bad shape, I quickly realized that the concept of "bad shape" is subjective. I was healthy as hell compared to most of the guys in there. The patient demographics broke down like this: almost all white, mostly under twenty-five years of age, and addicted to opiates. They might have been young, but they were wise beyond their years, in the sense that many had stared down the barrel of guns and watched helplessly as their friends died of overdoses. But for all that experience, they were immature. Most didn't care about the rules. A lot of them didn't want to be there—they were only in treatment to gain an advantage in their pending legal cases, so they called it "Junky Summer Camp."

The majority of staff were in recovery themselves. This made it easy for them to relate to most of the problems people were going through. I never had a problem with them, but I also followed their rules, even the ridiculous ones. I didn't mind getting up on time, making my bed, and showing up to the things I was supposed to go to.

A lot of the guys had problems with the staff and the treatment, which makes sense—they weren't there to heal. They didn't feel the pull, the drive to do something to transform their lives in a positive way. Like anything else, including jail, detox and rehab are only as useful as you make them. And I was committed to changing— to altering my course.

Every morning started with what I found to be the most helpful part of treatment: therapy, with a therapist leading a small group. It gave me the opportunity to share my experiences and feelings with a group that understood, listened, and could empathize. Where I grew up, you didn't talk about your feelings that much. And as I did this, I began to process what had happened, and I realized what I actually was running away from. It wasn't just the pain of losing my mother; it was the pain of something I felt had been a betrayal of her, her presence, and her devotion to me. I had always wanted to be a music teacher to follow in her path. But I hadn't even finished college, and I was in my thirties, living in her basement, DJing bar mitzvahs, and drinking until I couldn't see straight.

They had us do other things too, of course—recreational therapy, individual counseling, other small groups, lectures on basic life skills, mandatory AA or NA meetings, and the like. Some helped on my journey; some felt like bullshit babysitting. But one of the major sources of learning, in a way that surprised me, was the other patients. I learned way more than I thought I would from them. Many people had stories that were eerily similar to mine. Some people were in a much darker place than I as a result of their addictions, and I learned from them too. One of my biggest learnings from seeing addiction at its worst was that lying to myself was sabotaging my personal growth, and if I continued this type of sabotage, I was looking right in the face of what I was going to be, and I did not want that.

Over the course of my time in treatment, I went from feeling like a helpless weakling who wasn't ready to leave, to feeling content, missing my family, and feeling ready to leave. With each small breakthrough, I thought I had succeeded. Except, not even an hour after that little victory, I went back to thinking about drinking and pills, and feeling hopeless again. It was a cycle. I felt anxiety, real anxiety about my future—what I would do with this life, and how I would become a better parent. I learned a lot about how to live with anxiety, rather than drink it away.

Some patients found joy in my pain. They would laugh and make off-the-wall comments about me during some of the counseling sessions where everyone was asked to share. They would yell shit like, "Booze, some weed, and painkillers! Get the hell outta here!" I was a rookie, a novice in the area of addiction compared to most. Some were hardcore addicts of crack, heroin, cocaine, crystal meth, you name it, and they looked like it. Toothless and bony, with repugnant skin with open sores from the constant scratching all over their bodies and faces.

Luckily for me, the younger patients weren't interested in me, and I wasn't interested in them. I gravitated toward people who were closer to my age. They also had a track for people in my demographic: semi-functioning alcoholics in their thirties and forties who generally haven't lost everything (yet) as a result of their substance abuse. I was placed with that track for the bulk of my treatment; however, there was this one kid who truly tested my patience.

Some punk stole my sneakers three days into my stay, while I was sleeping. Everything in my body wanted to rip that kid from ear to ear, but I didn't. I had to remain focused. I was there to rid myself of problems, not add to them. He wasn't the greatest thief anyway, and I ended up finding my sneakers hidden on top of one of the dropped ceiling panels. Everyone encouraged me to fight, but there was no way I was going to allow myself to enter this place a free man and leave with a criminal charge.

I completed the program successfully in two weeks. Unlike a lot of the patients, I returned to my family. I felt good. My mind was clearer than it had ever been. My health was good, and I was grateful for what I had. I also attended outpatient treatment. I went to AA meetings for some time after, which I grew to enjoy. Against the recommendations of clinical staff, I did not search for a sponsor. I already had made up my mind, along with the motivation to stay clean. This was my turnaround. I had questioned everything that had led me to that point—my decisions and the motivations behind those decisions. I questioned where I was and where I wanted to go, and the type of father I wanted to be. I questioned my beliefs, my fears, why I did things, why I didn't do things, why I attracted certain people and circumstances, why I succeeded, and why I failed. I turned the very fabric of my life inside out and examined it in raw detail. It's from this point that I was able to build again, from the ground up, with a fresh perspective based on my renewed sense of clarity.

At the bottom, my patterns and behaviors had become glaringly obvious, and the triggers that kept me repeating those behavior patterns came into sharp focus. My mother, my biggest cheerleader, my idol, my superhero, my rock—was gone, and I was truly on my own. My dad and my sisters will agree, my mom had a super soft side for her only boy and stuck up for me even when I was wrong, and believe me, I was wrong a lot. I realized that hitting rock bottom was not only inevitable but necessary, because those behaviors were simply not conducive to my growth.

My mother's death forced me to hit my grown-up stride. On top of that, and perhaps most importantly, all the roles I'd played prior to her death popped into my conscious awareness, specifically the role of drug dealer, the rebel, and the know-it-all. It became clear to me that I'd been a kind of puppet, playing the same role over and over, creating the same dynamics over and over, and keeping the drama going over and over, like an actor in a soap opera. It's not until I broke the mold and started the journey back to my true self that I stopped playing those old, scratched records and began to create new conscious outcomes.

All these realizations led to me gaining humility. I saw that life was not black and white, and that I seriously didn't know everything. In fact, I realized that I knew very little, and I decided to become a student of life as well as a student in the classroom. I had been groomed to be a music teacher. It was time to become one. My mother died in June of 2010. By September, I was enrolled at Bridge-water State University to acquire my music degree.

In other words, I completely dropped my old life after detox. And this was as hard as it sounds: I was able to let go of everything because nothing was working anyway. Letting go of the old created space for the new, and soon after, new ideas, people, opportunities, talents, and gifts started to flood into my experience. And, it also meant that I let go of an old attitude. I stopped living like I was the victim of the white man. I had the power.

As I emptied my cup of the old version of Greg, I filled it back up with stuff that I actually wanted, instead of accepting what was unconsciously passed on to me. Historically, black people have been looked at as less than. As Ta-Nehisi Coates said, "It is truly horrible to understand yourself as the essential below of your country. It breaks too much of what we would like to think about ourselves, our lives, the world we move through and the people who surround us. The struggle to understand is our only advantage over this madness." I REPEAT, ONLY! Every black man who has somehow "made it" understands that this struggle is real. Think of it like this: Imagine you were running the Boston Marathon, and even when you crossed the finish line, you had to keep running. You broke through the tape, but the race wasn't over, and it was never going to be over.

I've known how black I am since as far back as I can remember. It's always been an issue. Whether I was the only black kid in the violin program in Hingham, Massachusetts, or the only black kid in the Episcopal Choir at St. Paul's in Brockton, or the only black kid in the Bridgewater University Chamber Group, or the only black music teacher an institution has ever had in Cambridge, Massachusetts, or the only one attending the *Jersey Boys* musical in Worcester, Massachusetts, just last week.

While I had to stop focusing on it in order to move forward and thrive, it was still there and it's with me every day. But, even with all the systemic racism and injustice, still, I recognized the need to accept full responsibility for all the outcomes in my life. I saw that blaming is counter-productive to success, complaining is useless, and making excuses is for the uninformed. I realized it was *I* who had created all the good and all the bad in my life. I dug the *hole* in which I was trapped, and only I could dig myself out of it in order to finally become *whole*. Which is why, as painful as it was, I now know I needed to hit rock bottom. And why I'll never stop being thankful for my mother—she always pushed me to be better, every moment of her life, and every moment after.

PART 2
THE LESSONS

4

Embrace the F*ck Up

"It's fine to celebrate success but it is more important
to heed the lessons of failure."

~ Bill Gates

We often talk about "easy" and "difficult" choices in life. Usually, the choices that seem easier in the moment are fictional. You decide to do something in an instant of weakness because it seems embarrassing or difficult to choose the option you know is better or right. For example, giving in to pressure to do something you would rather not do most likely will put you in a bad situation.

I have found myself in these moments many times. Choosing what looks like the easier option is a decision that often ends up leaving you feeling uncomfortable and trapped in a situation in which you have lost your integrity.

In the long run, the "easier" option is often harder and can lead to an inauthentic life.

I learned this lesson the hard way. At the age of nineteen, almost a year after my arrest, my mother brought me to the courthouse to turn myself in for sentencing. We walked in together: me acting calm, like the five-foot tough guy about to be hauled off to jail, while my mom looked like she could vomit at any moment. My dad stayed away from courthouses. "You made your bed," he used to say. For all his talk, my dad was no saint. He just happened to make it through the gauntlet of life unscathed by a serious encounter with the law.

The inside of the courtroom was just like the movies. My mom and I sat in the gallery surrounded by other convicts awaiting sentencing, some with families, some alone. I only remember this: the judge called out my name, read my sentence, and a man slapped cuffs on my hands. A door on the side of the courtroom opened, and I walked through it, guided by two officers, with my head hung low. This was when it stopped feeling like a movie. Usually, in the movies, they cut away after the door closes. But here I was, shackled to other men, walking down a long hallway toward the only future any of us could believe in: the county jail. That future, for the first time, felt real. And, as I moved farther from my past and from my mom, the fear I'd been feeling for a long time finally broke loose and overwhelmed me. I was going to jail, to be locked up with hundreds of other men, many of them potentially violent. If any of them found out how scared I was, I'd be dead.

Before we were sent to jail, we stopped off at the courthouse holding cells, which were just as dangerous. They were unsupervised, and the guards took off our cuffs before putting us in the cells. I got in and glanced around, scoping out potential threats, when I saw a face that shocked me: an acquaintance from Brockton, a kid straight from the projects, who we called Kevvy Kev. Now, Kevvy and I weren't close friends—we knew each other, ran in similar circles. But in that holding cell, where everybody else seemed like a threat, I felt like Kevvy and I were bosom brothers reunited. As soon as I saw him, I shouted his name, and he cut right toward me. We grabbed each other's right hands and wrapped our left arms around the other's torso. This was instant, an unmediated reflex. We pulled apart, and I instantly felt better. Here, I had an ally.

I'll never forget the next moment. Right after we pulled away, Kev looked at me and said, "Watch this." He jumped up as if bitten by a dog, and scanned the ten-by-ten holding cell. His gaze landed on this older white guy who was sitting there, doing absolutely nothing. Kevvy Kev got right in this helpless man's face and said, "What the fuck are you looking at?" Before the man could say one word, Kevvy Kev punched him dead in his face. For anyone with a soul, it was hard to watch. I had never been more happy to be friends with anyone than I was to be friends with

Kevvy Kev that day. See, he knew something none of us knew: you had to instill fear, right away, and get people talking.

After a while, they moved us to the county jail, and the whole way over, that poor white man just sat with his head way down, avoiding everyone's eyes. The thing people don't know about jail is this: it's easiest right when you get there, while you're being booked and processed. They herd you into a giant room, with rubber chairs and wood dividers, and a TV way up high in a plastic box, so nobody can touch it. Then you just wait for your turn to be fingerprinted and interviewed. It's a lot like the DMV. People think that's all that prison is: waiting. But that's not true. Once you're out of processing, in the actual day-to-day life of jail, you're battling to stay alive. When I was in processing, it was the last time I felt safe until after I got out. There, you're surrounded by Correctional Officers (COs), and that's not the punishment. The other inmates—that's the punishment.

After the holding cell, this felt like nothing, and I kept asking myself, "Is this real?"

I spent most of my time with my neck perched back as if I was in a barber chair getting a shave. The hard rubber chair chafed my neck at every move, and I wondered how many neck germs I was acquiring as I stared at the TV. The TV calmed me, but every now and then, I'd come back to reality and remember where I was headed.

We spent most of the day there, and in the early evening, COs came around with brown paper bags. Inside were sandwiches which contained pinkish meat with white and dark brown spots and a slice of stale cheese. It tasted like heaven.

After intake, they took us to a dorm that housed about a hundred inmates, and that's where we would wait for our final cell assignments. After sitting around the dorm for a day, this old woman came in and called my name. Moments later, I was sitting across a desk from her. She wore way too much makeup and smelled like a bottle of old perfume. She stared at me and shook her head back and forth. I felt like she was looking at me as if I was doomed. Finally, she asked me how I was feeling, and the floodgates of all the deepest fears, all the fears I'd been holding onto the last few days, opened. She was the only person I ever told how afraid I was, and I can't even remember her name. I can remember thinking that that meeting was my last chance, that if I didn't say this, nobody would know, and I'd never be saved.

I told this woman that I'd never been in trouble before, and just the thought of jail terrified me. It's a good thing I told her—from what I could tell she felt bad for me. She ended up sending me to a single-cell unit, which meant that I got an entire cell, complete with sink and toilet, to myself.

Once I arrived to the unit, the other inmates were on me like flies on shit. How the hell did you get sent to this unit? The single-cell unit is the most coveted unit in the entire jail. If you were sent to the single-cell unit, you either had some sort of connection on the inside, had been locked up for a while and displayed good behavior, or you probably snitched on someone and they were trying to keep you as safe as they could without sending you to protective custody. I was none of the above, but I was certainly not going to tell anyone I got sent there because I was scared, and the intake lady felt sorry for me. Instead, I just said, "Don't fucking worry about it."

Shortly after I arrived in jail, my mom came to visit. It was the classic thing—two phones and a sheet of glass. I got there before she did, which meant I watched her arrive. She came with the pastor of my church, and it was a good thing, too. When I tell you she could hardly walk for all her crying and shaking, I mean it. The pastor carried her toward me like she'd lost all her bones. As soon as I saw her, I instantly knew that she couldn't come back—it was simply too hard on her.

And it was hard on me too—I felt on the inside about as bad as she looked on the outside. Growing up, I'd always been so close to my mother, both emotionally and physically. I used to go up to her, put her in a headlock, and kiss her over and over again on the head while she told me to knock it off. But I couldn't hug her, couldn't smell her, couldn't even hear her real voice, only what came through the phone.

But worse than that, I could see her pain, and I knew it was my fault. I felt as bad as I would have if I had just stabbed her right in the stomach. I don't even remember what we talked about; I just remember that it was the first time I'd seen her in this much pain. Growing up, we think that our parents are invincible. We idolize them, make them into little gods, and here, I'd made my own mother mortal. I just wanted to shake and cry and hold her. But I was surrounded by all these other men, who, at the end of the hour, would stomp back into the lockup with me. So, instead, I leaned back and said, "Ma, knock it off."

I paid for that. Late at night, after she was gone and the sound from the other inmates had died, I sat there, crying silent tears. I'd seemed so callous, cold. She'd never know that I felt the same way she had, worse, maybe. I kept thinking about how my mother had poured so much into me, her first hope that I would take those musical and educational tools she'd forced into me and fashion a productive life for myself. She wanted goodness to feel natural to me. It didn't work. When she saw me on the other side of that glass partition, she realized that everything she'd poured into me had been poured away.

At that point, I still had eighteen months left on my sentence, and I didn't think that either of us could last that long. I needed a way to get out earlier. There were ways you could chip away at your time—get a job sweeping the floors, take a couple of classes, have good behavior. But, at most, that would knock a couple of months off. That wasn't going to cut it. I kept hearing other inmates talk about this boot camp—essentially, you had to apply for it, then they shipped you out to a camp. If you lasted eight months, they let you out the day you graduated, no matter how much time you had left. It was a gamble though—if you got kicked out, then they added another three months to your sentence, for "wasting the government's time."

In jail, it had a mixed reputation. A lot of guys thought it was fucked—they called it "modern slavery," because you did a bunch of work while white guys shouted at your face. And it was tough—eight months might sound like nothing next to eighteen, but people left for the camp only to come back a month later all the time.

But there were benefits—a lot of people said that it could completely change your life. And, everyone knew one thing about it: the food was a hell of a lot better there than in jail.

The only thing I cared about was getting out in eight months. It seemed like a no-brainer—either I'd spend eight months with a bunch of maniacs yelling at me, or eighteen sitting around locked up with a bunch of maniacs. That, and I was not supposed to be in jail. Yes, I committed a crime. But, "I" was not supposed to be in jail. I played the violin, for Christ's sake. At least, that's what I told myself, even though I hadn't picked up a violin in seven years. In those seven years, I had slipped so far. I was now surrounded by real criminals, career criminals. I ate with people who wouldn't hesitate to shoot you for not saying excuse me. Jail made me realize that, despite what I'd thought, I wasn't a true "thug." Yeah, I knew every verse to every one of 2Pac's songs. Yeah, I hung out with drug dealers, thieves, and gangbangers, but I was no thug. I surrounded myself with these types of people. I enjoyed "The Game." I gravitated to them like a bug to that very tempting neon light, and we all know what happens when the bug gets too close.

It was at this moment that I decided (unconsciously, I admit) to embrace my f*ck-up and face the music—which in this case meant boot camp.

I wanted out. I asked to apply, and a recruiter came out to interview me. Step one was to find out if I qualified for boot camp. Sentenced—check, under thirty—check, healthy—check, assault on a child—NO WAY. I was good to go.

Before I left, the recruiter gave me some advice: he told me it was Army style, that they were there to break men down and build them up again. He said I would be pushed beyond my limits, and that the only way to make it was to humble myself. Then the realest shit I ever heard came out of his mouth as if it was just another day at the office. He said, "Keep your eyes and ears open and your mouth shut!" I didn't really get what "keep your ears open" meant, until I got to boot camp. While the quote is from *Charlie and the Chocolate Factory*, it worked in jail as well.

The premise is this, and the rules are simple. Don't trust anyone, again ANYONE, in jail. Don't gamble, don't owe no one NOTHING. Give respect and expect it. If you are not a gangbanger, don't act like one. If you can't afford drugs or cigs, drop them. There is also a balance between being quiet and being scared to speak. If you are too loud, no one likes a loud mouth, but if you are too quiet, you may be suspected of being a child molester or something. Not my rules, but I had to follow them if I was going to survive.

The boot camp lived up to its reputation. It was hard, and everything turned on respect. Like in jail, you had to make sure that all of the other inmates respected you. If people knew that you could be disrespected without a fight, then you were buzzard meat. So you had to respect yourself and your peers, and make sure they respected you. Respect is something I never had a problem with. Being a little guy, it's what has carried me through this entire time. I always found the biggest, baddest mother-fucker I could find, and I made him my friend. Someone told me one time that a person is less likely to screw you over (or beat you up) if you know their family. That meant I would get to know this badass's mom, dad, brother, sister, grandma, whatever. There are a million houses still to this day that I can let myself into and give someone's mom a kiss as I enter their kitchen. It's always worked for me.

On top of that, unlike in jail, you had to respect the drill instructors. The fastest way to get your ass thrown to the curb was to stare down or talk back to the DIs. And they tried to bait you into it. On the very first day, I remember sitting around with all the other inmates, waiting to be processed, like in jail. There was this skinny Puerto Rican guy who looked wigged out, like he was in the middle of cocaine withdrawal. He kept telling us that he wasn't going to take any shit from the DIs. I thought to myself that this guy shouldn't have even gotten off the bus.

Sure enough, the DIs came in, and right away he was staring them down. Four dudes got up in his face and started shouting, and he didn't last a second. The coked-out kid shouted back, and pushed one of them. Then they were on his ass, and he was shipped back to jail before we even got our uniforms. Fortunately, I didn't have too much trouble with this type of respect, either. Growing up with my father, I got really good at being screamed at. It didn't take a lot to get him riled up in the first place, and I wasn't the easiest child to raise. He went off on me a lot, and whenever he would, I would just sit very still, very quiet, and act like I was listening. Of course, I wasn't listening. I mastered the art of being there without being present. So, no matter how much these guys shouted at me, I ended up being fine.

That wasn't their only demand, however. You always had to address them as sir twice, before and after anything you said. And you couldn't even talk without first asking to talk. I remember having to say, "Sir, this inmate requests permission to speak, sir." And you had to treat the other inmates with respect, and the DIs were watching you constantly.

The barracks were shaped like an L, with the DIs' office at the point where the two arms met. The office had big windows, and was always darker than the barracks, so they could be watching without you even knowing. They had rules for everything, and each rule had a different punishment if you broke it. My favorite: when two inmates got caught fighting, they had to carry around a giant log, one on each end, for the entire day after, sun up to sun down. These people would be walking around, carrying this heavy piece of wood, with someone that they hated.

Aside from that, they expected military precision from us. Each morning, they examined our beds and our gear. Our beds needed to be made military-style. Each of our shirts needed to be cleaned and pressed in a certain way, and our shoes had to have a certain level of shine. What amazed me was how well this all worked: I saw two guys who were in for attempted murder have a damn shoe shining contest. Some of the inmates loved it—they held themselves to a high standard for the first time in their lives, and thrived. We had heroin addicts who came in skinny and loopy and were buff and vivacious after three months. We had guys talking about enlisting when they got out of this thing.

It worked on me, too. I think there was some combination between seeing my mother in so much pain, and also in feeling like I was building myself up again in the boot camp, but I was resolved to make a better life for myself. The first time my dad, my sister, and my high school sweetheart, Ana, visited, I told them that.

Visits happened once every three weeks, in the mess hall, and the inmates had to sit with their backs to the chair, feet on the floor, and hands on their knees. My dad loved seeing me like that. I think he would have been happy to see me stay there for two or three years—as long as I was in camp, I couldn't be getting into trouble. And when I told them that, after this, I was going to clean up my act, they were looking at me with their fingers up their shirt, like, "Yeah, okay, Greg." I looked good, I sounded good, but none of them believed it would be my last time in jail.

My mom wanted to come and visit me while I was in boot camp, but I told her that I didn't think it was a good idea. After what happened when she visited in prison, I knew that she couldn't handle it, and I didn't want to put her through that pain again. My dad visited me in boot camp every chance he got. Growing up, he would dig into me while I got into trouble, and really rip into me right before I faced any big consequences, but once I was actually in the thick of things, he would always be there for me. And I appreciated that.

In fact, being in the boot camp made me love and appreciate my parents far more. I realized just how much they had done for me in my life. I heard so many horror stories in there. Some inmates never knew their parents; some inmates had parents who abused drugs and alcohol their entire lives. Some had abusive parents, and I was astonished.

Holy shit, I thought. *My parents were what every child wishes their parents were, and I still managed to find a way to fuck it up.* I often had to keep my mouth shut when inmates shared about their childhoods, because nothing I had to say seemed nearly as awful as the things people shared. I feared for my safety many times, feeling like some inmates looked at me as some sort of golden child. This was a legitimate concern—for all of the supervision, the boot camp was still a dangerous place. There were blind spots where the DIs couldn't see, or moments when everybody knew that the DI on duty was asleep or something, and you could get jumped. I saw guys walking around with weapons. At this place, I learned to be a light sleeper: we all slept in this big open room, and if somebody wanted to hurt you in your sleep, all they had to do was walk up to you.

There was one moment, one event, in my whole time at the boot camp when I felt I couldn't go any further. It wasn't waking up at 5:00 a.m., it wasn't getting yelled at, it wasn't the constant fear for my life, the long runs, the guards shutting the hot water off in the middle of our showers for no reason, or anything else they threw at us. It was 5:00 a.m. on Christmas Day, 1998. The barracks were cold. They were always cold—it was like living in a big tin can. I hated the cold. I laid there, still, on the top bunk with a wooly gray blanket that I tried to keep away from touching my face. It would have been completely dark, but the lights in the bathroom never went off. I was in the second-to-last bunk from the DIs' office, which meant I was fairly hidden from the office. The bad part is that I was the second closest to the bathrooms, which meant I slept with light in my face every night. It was a price I was willing to pay for not being at the front of the class. No complaining, remember?

That Christmas morning, I was exhausted. I'd literally cried myself to sleep the night before, and the sleep I fell into was fitful. Christmas Eve and Christmas Day were the two biggest days of the year for my family. They were the only times when everybody, all the aunts, uncles, cousins, siblings, in-laws, everyone, got together. Thoughts of my family chased each other through my mind all night. Nat King Cole's Christmas Album played over and over in my head. I could taste those little raspberry hard candies my mother could only find at Christmastime. I could smell the cinnamon, raisin, and walnut bread my mother would bake from scratch, only on Christmas. Being my mom's favorite (or at least I thought so), she knew I didn't like nuts in my food and would make me my own loaf with just cinnamon and raisins. I thought about that bread, the way it smelled like home. When I opened my eyes, I didn't see my mother's face, a table groaning beneath a feast. Instead, I saw the thirty inmates who had made it four months (we started with sixty) as little lumps of gray on their bunk beds.

That morning, all of the inmates in my barracks whispered Merry Christmas to each other and gave bro hugs as if we had been friends since kindergarten. Although this Christmas morning we were all behind bars, for a split-second, it felt real. It was a warm feeling that ended abruptly as some DI demanded that we "Get your ass outside for line-up!"

"Sir Yes Sir!" we screamed back.

There were multiple voices yelling, and all I could think of was how pissed these DIs must be that they were spending Christmas morning with a bunch of convicted felons. God help us. They put us through the ringer that day, but even while they did, I couldn't stop thinking about my family, and the love I'd once possessed from them. While my family all gathered together and celebrated, I ran for miles in the freezing air. At times, it felt almost like they didn't exist. And I didn't feel like I could talk to the other inmates about it. Some of these guys didn't know their parents; some were eating out of dumpsters right before they came to the boot camp. The entire day, I kept thinking, Just let me out. For twenty minutes. It felt like the fence and the camp and the DIs were strangling me. I couldn't think straight. I couldn't see past my own despair.

And this was one of those moments when I hated myself. I hated myself for putting myself in this controlled institution and situation. I couldn't go anywhere. And if I wanted that to change anytime soon, I'd have to endure much more than the cold air. And I did. When Graduation Day finally came, I was one of thirteen inmates who finished the program. We started with sixty, and out of the thirteen that finished, only ten of us were released and got to go home. The other three had had such serious charges prior to boot camp that their sentences had been shortened, but they still had to go back to county jail to finish their time. Some fell off the first day, two guys even made it to the week before graduation and decided they couldn't deal with each other anymore and started fighting, which was an automatic ejection from the program. I made it through because, unlike many of my fellow inmates, I was willing to stop the bullshit of making excuses or pretending that I ended up in jail by some sort of bad luck or mistake. It wasn't a mistake. I did it. And I was ready to move past it. But I couldn't move past it until I admitted and embraced the fact that I had fucked up. I put myself in jail because I did the crime, and I needed to expect more of myself. If you want to overcome your mistakes, thrive, and excel, you must embrace the fuck-up.

When I was released, it seemed like my mother had recovered from the jail blow—a brief but powerful intermission in my life that could have stolen my spirit, but it didn't. It just temporarily dimmed my shining light. Today, looking back at all that happened, I feel nothing but gratitude. No matter how painful, the experience helped me grow and question the system of values that I had been living by. Today, I know it was worth it. The decision I made to go to the boot camp gave me the discipline and courage to face life head-on, which enabled me to be who I am today.

5

Only Complain When It Counts

"Don't complain about things you're not willing to change."

~ Shivam Gupta

"Everyone in here is innocent," said Morgan Freeman's character Red, a convicted murderer, in *The Shawshank Redemption*. This is not just the stuff of fiction. When I was in jail, I realized just how true this was. Most of the black inmates I encountered not only believed they were innocent, but they believed they had more kindness, morality, self-control, generosity, and were more law-abiding than the people on the street. While, for most of the prisoners, it is highly unlikely that any of the above is true, I understand the impulse. I've been there. I know firsthand what it's like to be a black man in America behind bars. And when you're there, you have this strong desire, need even, to see yourself in a positive light. Because everyone around you—the guards, society, the judges, cops, everyone—does everything in their power to cast you in a negative light. They tear you down. So you have to find a way to keep some sense of self-esteem, or you'll never make it.

This is why I got caught up in the same complaining parties as everybody else, even though I knew that it was my fault I was in jail. It usually went like this: a group of guys would get together and talk about their arrests, insist they were innocent, and tell stories about how fucked up the cops were and how they got screwed over. It eventually became a game of one-upmanship. If someone complained about the details of their arrest, I had to find something to outdo their complaint, to prove to them and myself that I was even more wronged than they were, even more innocent, and an even better person. In essence, I was complaining about nothing. I was stretching reality to the breaking point, but at the time, it was just as important to survival as air and water.

Of course, we were just blowing off steam. We weren't doing anything productive by complaining. Most of us were guilty, and we damn well knew it. In the end, all of our complaining added up to nothing. We were just making excuses for ourselves, and it wasn't getting us anywhere. And you know how I feel about excuses.

That being said, there are times when you need to complain, to speak out and make your voice heard, in the face of some injustice. This type of complaining is deeply intertwined with our culture at large. Almost every major public achievement that we, as Americans, can feel proud about—starting with the revolution itself, through the end of slavery, the expansion of the franchise, and civil rights as a whole—all stemmed from these sorts of complaints. So, you need to use your voice when it counts.

Silencing Myself

One day, in 2014, my first year teaching music at a very prestigious school, and fifteen years out of jail, my stomach was in excruciating pain. I'm not one to complain, so I suffered through a few classes, trying to hide it. Apparently, I failed, because when I bumped into my boss, she took one look at me and said, "Get out of here, go home."

I told her I was okay, I could make it through the rest of the day, and it was no problem. But she insisted that I go. So I packed up my things and walked to the bus stop about two hundred yards from the school. I took the Seventy-Two down Concord Street all the way to Harvard Square. I hopped off the bus and walked very slowly down the ramp to the redline train. My stomach pain was getting worse and worse. Seven stops later, I was at South Station. After all that, I was only halfway home.

The fancy school was in Cambridge, well secluded from the rough parts of Brockton I still called home. When I got to South Station, I had about twenty minutes or so to wait before the commuter rail train left for Brockton.

By this time, my stomach hurt so bad that I couldn't sit still, so I paced back-and-forth, essentially across the station. The whole time, I felt like there were eyes on me. I scanned the entire place like a young buffalo on the lookout for a pack of wolves, and I made eye contact with three or four different white guys. My black antennas went up, and believe me when I tell you, I knew something was about to go down.

I was right. Seconds later, I was completely surrounded. It looked like a scene out of one of those super gangster action movies where they finally corner the bad guy, guns drawn, barrels pointed straight at his face, and oh yeah, with barking dogs as well. But it was reality, and apparently, I was the "bad guy." I remember seeing a swirl of bulletproof vests with lots of little pockets that looked like they were holding grenades, and hearing the German shepherds' barking echo off the cement ceilings and walls.

I was so pissed, I wanted to swing at the cops and SWAT teams surrounding me. But, luckily, my stomach hurt so bad there was not going to be a physical reaction from me. Above all of the shouting and barking, I remember yelling, "Can I fucking help you?" Then, like every black man in a terrible situation, I kept asking why the hell am I being surrounded? Finally one cop gave me an answer: I'd been stopped because I looked suspicious.

What's crazy is, I was in my school clothes. Now, sure, they weren't as preppy as what most of my white colleagues wore, but still, I looked professional. My attire happened to be a style that I like to call "funky-hip-brown-music-teacher-fresh-fly." Still, as funky fresh and fly as I looked, I still looked like a teacher.

Looking back on it, I think part of the problem was that this encounter came just about a month after the Boston Marathon bombing. Of course, I had on a backpack, and at that time in Boston, any brown person with a backpack became a danger in the eyes of the police. All the same, I think I looked a lot less like a terrorist and a lot more like Richard Dreyfuss in *Mr. Holland's Opus*—if Mr. Holland had been black and had a stomachache.

So, I was surrounded, and they started asking, well, more like shouting, all these questions at me, like *what's your name, where are you going, where are you coming from?* Blah blah blah.

I was furious but managed to keep my head enough to pull out my phone and let everyone know that I was filming. Eventually, though, the anger inside of me found its way out of my mouth, and I went off like a drunken sailor. I want to say I got real black on them, but this was one of those times when I don't think it was about how I felt as a black man. This was about how I felt as a human being. I was sick as a fucking dog, and I was being surrounded with guns pointed at me for absolutely nothing.

Then, as a final straw, one of them asked, "Why do you have a book bag?"

To which I replied, "Didn't I just tell you? I'm a fucking music teacher! I have books in my bag, asshole, what do you think I have in my bag?"

I don't think that was a completely inappropriate answer for the circumstances I was in. He answered back, "Do you speak to your students with that mouth?"

I've never wanted to hit a cop so badly.

*   *   *   *

After I'd answered all of their stupid questions, they didn't even have the desire to search my bag. In a way, that kind of pissed me off even more. Little by little, each of the soldiers, cops, and SWAT team members faded away. When one of them handed me back my ID and said that I didn't have any warrants and I was good to go, this infuriated me even more because of the amount of force with which they came at me.

To make this perfect, the last thing he said to me was, "Have a good day."

After it all, I was so angry, so jittery, and so shot through with adrenaline, that I almost forgot about my stomachache. I finally got on the commuter rail and called one of my best friends, Steve Siagel. Besides being prominent and successful, he also happens to be Jewish, which is part of the reason why I called him. I honestly feel that Jewish people are much closer to understanding what it's like to be black in America, in the sense that a group of people tried to exterminate them at one time just like a group of people tried to enslave us.

I told Steve the whole story. I was pissed, and I needed an ally's ear, someone to hear me complain. I wanted and even expected him to tell me that our next step was to call the news stations and put this injustice on full blast. I wanted this splashed beneath the BREAKING NEWS banner on CNN for the entire weekend. The world needed to know what had happened.

Steve heard me out, offered his shoulder for a second, and then he asked me a question I will never forget: *Do you really want to risk your job?*

He went on to tell me that I should think about this before I call the news. He asked if I thought it would cause me more of a headache than a win, with this being my first year at such an amazing institution?

My first thought was, "Steve you're such a pussy, always taking the easy way out." God knows I would never say this to him because I love him too much, but I thought it.

So in this case, I asked myself, *Would I be speaking up? Or would I just be complaining?* We are all guilty of complaining about stupid little problems.

But what happened at South Street Station was NOT a little problem; it was a stupid problem, but not a little one.

I mean, it's always a stupid problem when cops have an overreaction to some innocent action of a black person. As Ta-Nehisi Coates ponders in *Between the World and Me*, "How do I live free in this black body when this black body already has its predetermined spot in the 'American Dream?'"

I spent a long time reflecting on what had happened. In truth, it brought to the surface something that I had felt for a long time: I was trapped between two worlds. On the one hand, I was the staff music teacher at one of the most elite high schools in the country. On the other, I was a former crack dealer, born, bred, and still rooted down in one of the toughest parts of Boston. Even if everything I did, the way I lived, carried myself, and dressed for work every day put me in the first category, the world would still treat me as part of the second. And as hard and painful as straddling these two worlds could be, I didn't want to lose the foothold I had at this school. So I ended up burying the incident and acting like it never happened.

But it did.

I still feel conflicted about the fact that I let Steve talk me off the ledge, simply because I was afraid that by complaining, I could lose my job. The fact that I felt like I was vulnerable to losing my job for complaining in the first place is also something to complain about. We all know this situation would have been handled differently had I been a white guy. We all can imagine the outrage if the cops had behaved that way toward a white man wearing a backpack at South Street Station. But, looking back on it, this was a moment when I wish I had spoken up. Especially because, as I would learn later, no matter how tightly I clung to my position at the school, they would never stop seeing me as the black kid from Brockton.

BREAKING MY OWN SILENCE

While I was working at the same school, also in my first year there, one of the veterans, a Muslim black man, sat me down and gave me "The Talk." Essentially, he wanted to give me pointers on how to navigate being a person of color on staff at this elite white school. Then, he said one thing that stuck to me more than anything else: "One day, this institution will let you know exactly how black you are."

His saying this was what went through my head when I decided not to file a formal complaint about the train station incident. I believe I thought I could at least delay, if not avoid, the institution showing me how black I was.

In a way, I think part of why I was hired was because I was black. I don't mean like affirmative action, just that I was hired at this institution to bring a new flavor to the music program. The music teacher before me had been there for more than two decades.

After my second year, we received a new Head of School, who came in with great energy, a huge commitment to creating a greater sense of community, and tons of liberal ideas. Almost all of the faculty, myself included, were excited about the new Head. Right off the bat, I connected with her commitment to bring people within the school community closer together. This institution was separated into three schools, a lower, middle, and upper school. There was a noticeable disconnect between the three, and she wanted to strengthen the bonds between them.

My lifelong dream of directing a massive choir had never ceased, and I saw this as the perfect opportunity to create this choir, show my support for the new Head, and make a great impression. So I did it, and created a choir of eighty-five singers, twenty-three of whom were faculty/staff, and the remaining sixty-two were students ranging from preschool to twelfth grade. We performed at the new Head's induction, and it was the first time the school had formed any performance group this large. The choir got a standing ovation once we finished our rendition of "Put A Little Love In Your Heart."

Two months later, in December, while watching the evening news, I got an idea for another way to improve community connections. I saw a story about a firefighter who was hitting the streets, dressed in a Christmas elf costume and carrying two pillows. He would approach random people, hand the person one pillow, and then proceed to have a very gentle pillow fight with them. Clip after clip, there was this grown man in an elf suit laughing, smiling, and having pure fun with people he didn't even know. When asked why he was doing this, he responded that he just wanted to do something nice for people during the holidays, to make them smile. A random act of kindness. I instantly wanted to make my students a part of this. I posted something on Facebook, asking for help getting in contact with the firefighter. For all its size, Boston seems small at times, and within days, I had his girlfriend's email.

In a few emails to the firefighter, I explained my vision, and he agreed to come to my school and participate in my master plan. I organized a flash mob pillow fight with my students and the new Head of School. All parties met in my classroom one day, and my students were AMAZED that I somehow got this famous elf, who was the talk of Boston, to come to our school. The students who participated varied in age. Some students were as young as eight and some as old as thirteen, so, to them, this was like meeting President Obama would have been for me. I also reached out to the local news station, and they were more than happy to send a film crew to document the entire thing. I armed my students and the new Head of School with pillows and hand-held bubble machines. We walked to the middle school during their lunch period and stormed their lunchroom, bombarding them with bubbles, and we had the most fun pillow fight in school history. The news crew caught everything, and we were the lead story that night on the seven o'clock news. Four months into the new Head's maiden voyage, and there she was, on the evening news, spreading holiday cheer with the city's most privileged kids and her one black music teacher.

This happened on a Tuesday. Three days later, at 10 a.m. the Friday before the start of our two-and-a-half-week winter break, I sat at my desk feeling great about myself. I had created a schoolwide choir that was eighty-plus members strong, I'd gotten the new Head some great publicity, and I had a few other major accomplishments notched up in the first semester. I also had a meeting at noon with the new Head to discuss a salary increase.

Then, my boss, Director of the Lower School, walked into my classroom and said that I needed to follow him to his office right now. My boss and I were friendly, but this day he walked in front of me, leading me to his office, instead of walking with me and conversing as we usually did. I knew something was up, but I had no idea what I was about to walk into.

When I entered his office, I found the new Head and a member of the Human Resources office, waiting with stern faces. The new Head came right out and said, "Greg, this is about to be a difficult conversation." Then, she asked if I had shown a twenty-minute PBS documentary on The Harlem Renaissance to a fifth grade class three weeks prior.

I said yes, not seeing why there would be a problem. These are the same fifth grade students who do a project on the civil rights movement, where they look for newspaper articles from that time period. Of course, they end up seeing images of black men hanging from trees, and they put these in their presentations. I couldn't figure out anything that would pop up in a twenty-minute PBS documentary about the Harlem Renaissance that could be more vulgar or disturbing than what they'd already seen.

The new Head went on to tell me that *one* parent had had an issue with the video, and this parent had claimed the video was "inappropriate" for her child.

I disagreed, and that did not sit well with the new Head. I could tell from the look on her face that she was used to people just conforming to what she wanted. An eerie feeling crept up my spine and made the hairs on my arms stand at attention. The kind of feeling you get when you are about to get into your first fight on the playground.

I stood my ground, explained my lesson plans, explained the two weeks of discussions that preceded the video, shared exactly what was shown, and what was discussed after the video. All of that meant absolutely nothing. All the time I'd put into preparing this specific lesson meant nothing. The new Head put me on administrative leave for the following two weeks. After which, she informed me, there would be a meeting to discuss my future at this institution.

I felt this tremendous loss in that moment. I was not told who the parent was that complained, but they must have been very powerful. For any Head of School to take the lead on a situation like this is unheard of. Usually, this sort of thing got handled by a Director of a school. To add insult to injury, the new Head confiscated my computer and laptop, took my keys to my classroom, and told my children (who were enrolled in the school) and me that we all had to leave the premises immediately.

All she said was, "I'll be in touch," and walked out the door.

No apologies, no acknowledgment of the ridiculousness of the situation or of my diligence as an educator. I can't remember how I went from standing to sitting, but I ended up on the floor, crying, with my arms wrapped around my legs and my head buried between my knees. My head was too heavy to carry. I have to be honest, I expected a hand to land on my shoulder and a voice to say, "Everything will be okay." But all I heard were footsteps, as the HR woman and my boss followed the new Head out of the room. When they closed the door, it slammed shut like a cell door at count time. When I lifted my head, I was all alone, in silence.

What just happened?

My boss came back in a few minutes later. He walked with me back to my classroom, not in front of me like he had twenty minutes earlier. I was a complete mess and had to stop, kneel to the ground, and catch my breath a few times on the short walk back. To make things worse, I had to listen to my boss tell me how messed up he thought this situation was. He had the audacity to tell me that he was pissed about the way the new Head had spoken to me, her timing (the day before our winter break and two hours before my salary increase meeting), and her entire handling of the situation.

Eventually, I told him to stop. Everything he was telling me was what he should have said in the moment to her face. Telling me after the fact meant nothing. Standing up for what he claimed to believe in and confronting the beast at the time of the beast-ing was the right thing to do, and he'd failed as miserably as had I with the South Station incident.

Once we arrived at my classroom, he continued to talk, and I can't tell you one thing he said. I was in a daze, confused, devastated, angry, sad, upset. All of a sudden, my son and daughter came walking into my room. I looked a hot mess, and now I was face to face with my children. My lowest moment. When my children saw me, they began to cry. They were clueless, but they knew something was wrong with Daddy. Zoe was nine and Zion was five at the time. Without my permission or knowledge, the administration had taken it upon themselves to remove my children from their classrooms, bring them to me, and escort us to a car they'd arranged to get us off the property.

I felt like a criminal. We were paraded through the campus, leaving the people who saw us to make up their own stories as to what they were witnessing. Walking through the campus that day, to this arranged vehicle, reminded me of the day I went to jail, twenty years prior.

It felt exactly like when they slapped the cuffs on my wrists and led me down that secret hallway. The one that no one knows where it leads into the future, except this time, I was holding my children and wondering how I was going to explain to them what was happening.

I felt like a black man in America, not the accomplished, outstanding African American music educator I felt like moments before that meeting. I was humiliated. I don't know how I held it together, but I couldn't let my children see me crumble when in all actuality, I was crumbling inside.

That veteran Muslim teacher was right. This institution not only let me know how black I was, they let my children know as well.

At the end of my two-week leave of absence, we had a meeting to decide my future at this school. It was the same cast of characters as the last meeting. Again, no one spoke but the Head of School. This meeting was like boot camp all over again, but this time it just didn't feel right. I had done nothing wrong; I had no debt to pay. The Head sat at the far end of a long table. The only thing missing was a robe and a gavel.

The way she spoke, the tone of her voice, and her body language displayed dominance as I sunk in my chair. I'm not the most polished or professional individual around, but I know when my body tells me that something isn't right, and I could see the other two people in the room felt it as well. I was under attack.

During this meeting, the new Head harassed me, said embarrassing things to me and about me, and lied about me, like accusing me of stealing a school computer when someone else had stolen it out of my car. She even presented me with false, invalid documents. She was vicious. I wasn't the only one who felt this way. Halfway through the meeting, the representative from HR stood up, shouted "STOP!" and asked the new Head what any of this had to do with the twenty-minute PBS documentary, and to please move on. Even she couldn't sit through the gauntlet of humiliation this new Head was putting me through. Again, my immediate boss sat in silence.

After about a half-hour of this madness, she closed her folder and told me she was going to give me one more chance, as if she was doing me a favor, and said she really wanted to keep me employed at this institution. I was in total shock, and rightfully so. She'd called me a liar, a thief, and a bad person, and after all that, she had the audacity to ask me how we move forward from here. There was a long moment of silence as everyone in the room tried to comprehend what was taking place.

She then told me that although I just finished a two-week leave of absence, I was going to be suspended for a week without pay, and I was also given a last-chance agreement with very strict rules and guidelines to follow. I would have to:

1. Work under a mentor to design my lesson plans.

2. Be observed teaching eight times in five months, unannounced by the Head of School, the Director and the Assistant Director.

3. Take off-campus classes for better teaching skills.

4. Have all videos shown pre-approved by the Director.

5. Act in a professional manner.

And my favorite . . .

6. Release all my rights to bring a lawsuit against this institution.

While this was a lot to take in, it got worse. Before we said our final goodbyes, she felt the need to give me one last bit of information. She told me that regardless of the outcome, whether I stay or not, my children would always have a home there. She claimed that they were valued members of the community, and they would be able to remain at that institution for the remainder of their schooling through twelfth grade. Was she searching for a thank you? Was I supposed to be grateful? Were my children valued members of the community when she dismissed them from class and had them escorted off the premises?

The new Head handed me a copy of this agreement and told me I had a couple of days to review it. I would not be allowed to come back to work without signing it. And just like the group of renegade cops at the South Street Station, she shook my hand and said, "Have a good day."

I walked out of that meeting feeling as if I'd just attended my own roast. I felt abused, beat down, discriminated against, and less than human. In my eyes, the rules and guidelines were unreasonable, unreachable, and straight-up insulting. I also felt there was something very wrong about that meeting. There was no way a person in her position should be able to talk to a human being the way she had spoken to me. Furthermore, the accusations, the false documents, the lies, the embarrassment, the humiliation, the optics of parading a black family being escorted off campus by the white guard, the dismissal of my children from class—all of it just didn't feel right.

I consulted a lawyer, who agreed, and informed me that I had a very strong case should I choose to take legal action. The new Head had broken laws. This time, I decided to speak up. I realized that if I didn't, if I just acquiesced, I would not be living according to my values. I wouldn't be standing up for what I believed and taking action in that direction. I realized that my children would be watching.

I requested a meeting with Human Resources to review my options and everything that had happened from the first meeting to the present. It was no longer about the PBS video. Inappropriateness is totally subjective, and remember, I worked for a wealthy and powerful group of parents, so whoever had a problem with the twenty-minute PBS documentary on the Harlem Renaissance had way more time and money to argue about that than I did. I had already decided to let that fight go.

My beef was about everything that happened after that. When the HR representative met with me and I explained my story, she agreed with my concerns and said that she thought the new Head was way out of line. She specifically recalled how uncomfortable she'd felt sitting at that table listening to the Head tear me to shreds. She admitted that she was about to burst when she stood up and yelled, "STOP!" She then said that she would go back to her superiors and relay my concerns and requests.

Less than a week later, she returned and said that all of my requests were denied. My concerns would not be considered, and she said that it would, "Not be in my best interest" to pursue any legal action against the new Head. After being threatened by HR about taking further action, I knew it was time for me to leave this institution. I had to speak up, and I wasn't going to give up everything I believed in just to cling to a job in a community that didn't welcome me. I learned my lesson from the train station.

I didn't complain about the train station incident because, at the time, it didn't count. Let's be real, no one would give a shit about another black guy getting harassed by law enforcement, and I had just begun my dream job with great pay, at a well-respected school that offered me a chance to be looked at differently than I'd ever been viewed before. When people heard the name of this institution, it demanded respect and admiration, and I was their music teacher—everything I'd ever wanted.

After the train station incident, it seemed that the risks of speaking up outweighed the risks of not speaking up. But with the treatment I'd received at this school, I could not tolerate this act of injustice. Not this time.

Holding back from speaking up or waiting to be asked to speak serves no one. This is because our voice carries greater meaning than just the words. It carries our convictions, our passion, or our lack of passion. It conveys more about who we are as people. In order to advance in any area, our thinking must be seen and heard.

I accept my mistakes, and I don't make excuses for them. That means that I expect the same from other people, and I refuse to make excuses for other people's mistakes. I'm not going to say that it's understandable or justifiable to sic a SWAT team and K-9 unit on me because I was pacing and wearing a backpack right after the Boston Marathon bombing. Nor is it okay that one rich parent has the power to pressure a Head of School to do what the parent wants, even if the parent is a big donor to the school.

All the same, I do feel a bit of empathy for the Head of School. She came in with so much enthusiasm about retaining teachers of color, and so much energy, and was so kind to me at the beginning, that I have to believe her hand was forced. It just doesn't make sense any other way.

Yet I cannot excuse her behavior. The name of this book is "Excuse Limit Zero," not "Mistake Limit Zero." It's not about us having to hide our mistakes, or pretending that we never make them. It's that we have to think about our mistakes from an empowered place, which means we don't pretend that it's not our fault. We don't make excuses for our results. We just own them.

And I've learned that when you do complain, make sure it's about something that matters. I left that job, and it was scary. But it was the right choice. I've since been hired by another elite school, and when I tell this story, my peers and supervisors commend me for having the bravery to stand up for what I believed in. In the long run, standing up for yourself and what you believe in always will serve you better.

6

USE EVERYTHING

"Some people want it to happen, some wish it would happen, others make it happen."
~ Michael Jordan

I almost didn't write this chapter, because none of the stories you are about to read has a Hollywood ending. There was no grand performance, no throngs of crying and grateful parents, no proud faces of accomplished children, no flowers, no press, no curtain call. Nor do these stories include blaring cop lights, barking dogs, or shadowy and intimidating prisoners. These stories aren't the most exciting or dramatic. But they don't need to be. Because the massive heartwarming endings, the big successes and accomplishments, are made out of nothing more than our small day-to-day choices. Great moments, if they happen at all, are born from our ability to use what's around us. And that's what these stories are about:

using everything to get us closer to our goals. Because *Excuse Limit Zero* means that we can always find what we need when we need it.

Growing up, my mom would tell me about when she was a student at Boston University (BU), and every Saturday, she would take kids from the church and local housing projects to the swimming pool at BU. She was a charmer and could charm anyone. She would charm the guard at the pool to let them in, charm all her dorm mates into letting these kids use their bikes, and charm the people on the T to let all the kids ride free. The world was her "stockroom." It was plain to see that she was dead serious about these unprivileged kids, so it was hard to say no to her.

Like so many other things, I inherited this passion from my mother. And, in 2011, I followed that passion until I ended up scrambling to set up a stage in the lunchroom of the Neighborhood House Charter School. The place reeked of spoiled milk and trash. The acoustics were terrible, but we were ready anyway. I had organized a short performance of African drumming, singing, and dramatic dance by fifteen kids from the after-school program. Parents began to fill the seats and most wore a look of, "What the hell am I doing here in the middle of the day?" plastered on their faces. The cafeteria was structured like the basement of a parking garage, so we had to work hard to place the stage and chairs in just the right spots so everyone could see, but still people moved and maneuvered their chairs to get a better view.

The air was electric. The girls had their hair and makeup done, the boys were walking around tall and proud, smiles as wide as their faces could stretch. This was their Carnegie Hall. I'd even thrown together some costumes, which were awful. I mean, we worked our magic to make them presentable, but they were awful by any standard of school I've ever worked in. Still, the kids wore them like they'd been sewn by Gucci himself, and their pride made the costumes look good.

At this time, I had already been working for Siagel Productions and Event Planning as a bar mitzvah MC, and I had some clout with the warehouse guys, so I could borrow whatever I needed to make our venue look amazing. There's only so much you can do with a lunchroom, but we did it all. I borrowed the black pipe and drape set to box in the stage in order to make it look like an auditorium. I had up-lights on every beam along the walls, because it's not a show without lights, right? Since there were no shades to pull down, we used black construction paper to cover the windows and darken the room.

We pulled out all the stops because it was a momentous occasion. Somehow, I had pulled together the first-ever performance given by the after-school kids in this program that included dancing, singing, and a little bit of drama.

Things weren't perfect, and I could have done more with more money, of course. But why complain? When working in the inner-city school system, you either make things happen or you complain to deaf ears. I chose the former, and the kids gave one hell of a performance.

Regardless of what stops you from achieving more, one thing is certain: making things happen will start with you. As you shift your current state of mind, understanding that you are in the driver's seat, you quickly realize that anything is possible.

When I wrote that this chapter did not contain a grand performance, I was telling the truth. We did present a performance, but it was not grand in any sense of the word. It's so much easier to blame others or our circumstances instead of taking responsibility, even in situations where we actually win. It may not feel like a win, but nevertheless, it's a win. I had to realize that I'm unique with my own sense of purpose, so I had to ask myself, *what is it that motivates me, makes me optimistic, and provides a sense of meaning?* Teaching kids is what I do, turning nothing into something is what I do. It's what my mother taught me a long time ago. It always guides me to the heart of my inner motivation. Any time you can get kids to express themselves and to enjoy, learn, and perform an art, it's always a win.

* * * *

There are few places where resourcefulness is more necessary than in an inner-city school. Part of that is because there is never enough money to hire enough staff, so you have to pick up the slack. I had many jobs at the Neighborhood House Charter School. I was a substitute teacher, the after-school music instructor, a teacher's aide, and I helped out the math teacher during the summer-school program. One of the many menial jobs I had was to clean out a closet in the music teachers' classroom. No one gave me this job, but I took it on after someone asked if I could grab something out of the closet, and it was so messy that I decided to clean it.

After I'd been cleaning awhile, I noticed lots of green violin cases hidden in the back of the closet. My heart stopped. I couldn't believe what I was looking at. I forced my way to the back of the closet, pushing stuff out of the way until I was standing in front of this massive wall of dusty violin cases.

I rummaged through the cases, opening each one to see what treasures they held. Most of the violins were old, broken, and mostly useless. Their bow hair was frazzled just like the hair on one of my sister's dolls that she'd forgotten about for years at the back of her closet.

But, as I searched, I started to find some that were salvageable. The first thing that came into my head was, "I've got something here." I went to the music teacher and asked why she had all these violins in the back of the closet. She said they'd been there forever; there used to be a violin program here, but it had died out a long time ago. No one had touched them for a while, and she hadn't found the time to do anything with them.

In my mind, no matter how broken these instruments were, they could still be useful. These violins had remained stashed away because people focused on the problem instead of looking for a solution.

I let her know that I was a violinist and had been playing since I was three years old. I asked if I could inspect them all to see what shape they were in. She told me that all of the violins were trash, but I was welcome to check anyway. I think she truly thought I wasn't going to be able to make anything work, but she didn't know me very well. I went back to inspect the violins more closely and I found that, while most of them were beyond saving, there were at least ten that I could get repaired enough to play, eventually.

Nothing was ready to be played at that moment, but I knew I could do something. I went to my boss and told her that I wanted to start a violin program during the after-school program. I had a great rapport with the students at the Neighborhood House. The kids thought I was cool and they would follow my lead. If I wanted them to sing, I always had a bunch of kids who would join my choir. If I was teaching dance, I had a bunch of kids who wanted to be in my dance class. I knew it wouldn't be hard to find kids to join my violin program. My boss agreed and gave me the okay to start the program.

But like I said, the violins were not ready to be played, so I had to do something until I could finish the repairs. So I went to the art teacher, who also happened to be the head of the music department at the school. I'd had experience with papier-mâché because my mother, being one of the most frugal people I know, was always creating things with papier-mâché instead of buying them.

I asked the art teacher if we could make papier-mâché violins and bows so I could at least start to train the kids on how to hold the violin, hold the bow, and start using their fingers. These were all the small, important details required to begin violin training. She thought this was an amazing idea. This also happened to get me more hours at the school, which made me more money—a welcome side effect. Now I would come into the school during the school day, and in the art class, I would help the art teacher and the students make these papier-mâché violins and bows. I've always found that when kids invest time into creating something, they are more apt to be excited about the final product because of their time invested in creating it.

I ended up recruiting ten students (all boys, though that wasn't my intention) to join my violin ensemble. I don't think every kid truly understood what they were signing up for, but because it was with Mr. Greg, they were in. Most of these boys had never even seen a violin in person, never mind touched one. I feel safe in saying that most of them probably had never heard the sound of a violin.

As we worked on these papier-mâché violins, I saw their excitement grow, I could feel it. To capitalize on that excitement, I would show the students videos of violinists playing hip-hop music—black violinists. Everyone wanted to be like the guys in the videos because they looked like them, and the music was familiar. I've always found that once you get the kids on your side, or you get them excited about something, they will do anything and everything you ask them to do. So, my pedagogy always goes like this: first, get them on your side, then you can work the educational aspect into the activities without them even realizing it.

The violin ensemble never made it to performance status, but the experience was priceless for them and for me. I remember seeing them in the hallways, carrying their violin cases, prouder than ever. At the time my violin ensemble got started, I happened to be in the middle of my search for a full-time teaching position, and I was close. I had many applications filled out and many interviews lined up, so it was only a matter of time, but that did not stop my determination to make this happen. And here is how.

I knew I had to start small. Changing the world won't happen overnight. Each and every day, I took small steps toward a more positive and bigger goal. Each small action encouraged bigger results and built my confidence. I also had to visualize my goal. Do you often dream about what could be? You have the power to make those dreams a reality.

As soon as I saw those violins in the back of that closet, I knew what I wanted, the same way I knew where I wanted to be in life. This thinking acted as my guiding light and gave me a sense of optimism. Lastly, I stayed true to my authentic self even when life tried to change me into someone I wasn't or tried to deter me from making something amazing happen. I needed to listen to my inner voice. No matter what, always stay true to your core values, take risks, and surround yourself with inspiring people.

I ended up getting an amazing job before we got the violins repaired, and I left the Neighborhood House Charter School. There was no one left to continue the program, and it fell apart. I had no faith that anyone would continue it, but that didn't stop me from taking the journey.

Again, no Hollywood ending, but I came, I saw, and I did my best with what I had. I was disappointed that we didn't get the program up and running before I left, but I believe it was still worth pursuing. For the few months the program lasted, I truly believe it changed those boys and their view of the violin, and more importantly, the view of a black man who looks and talks like them and plays a violin. As a result, I can say with confidence that this was one of the most rewarding experiences of my life and also one of my biggest accomplishments.

When life doesn't turn out the way we'd hoped, planned, or expected, it's easy to feel tremendous disappointment and start doubting everything, including ourselves. However, your disappointment might be the best thing that has ever happened to you. You never know what door or opportunities may open up for you. Who knows, you might not even end up being who you expected to be. But still, you went for it, and in the end, that's what counts.

At about the same time I put together the violin ensemble in 2011, I decided to put together a Brockton city-wide chorus, mainly because I was only working part time during the week and on weekends, and I had time. It had long been my dream to direct something like the Boston City Singers, a chorus that would highlight the voices of my community, and I felt like now was the right time. I had no money, no support, and no one to help me out. I was on my own, but I believed I could do it. The first step was to list all the things I needed to make it happen: I needed a place to rehearse, I needed to get the word out, I needed to start recruiting kids and a piano, along with a pianist. This place did not have a piano, so it looked like we were going to have to make do with an electric keyboard. I wasn't happy about it, so I ended up digging mine out of storage, and that's what we used.

I was (and still am) a member of the Brockton Protectors Club, a private, nonprofit club in a residential neighborhood, started many years ago by a few Brockton firefighters. It's a simple place: dirty, dusty, and pretty much exactly as you would imagine a firefighters' drinking headquarters would look. There's wood paneling everywhere, old bar stools, and an endless number of names carved into the bar. There's a huge parking lot in the back of the building, and people use that entrance. I'm willing to bet that ninety-nine out of a hundred people would drive right by this place and have no idea what it is. It's no five-star bar, but it's home, a place where everyone knows your name.

For the longest time, I'd been hanging out there thinking that it only had one floor. Then, one day, I overheard someone ask for the key to go upstairs. It turns out there was a function hall up there. Once I heard that there was an upstairs, something clicked. I saw that was a potential asset, the first piece of the puzzle I could put in place. What my mother always taught me proved to be true. When you have your mind set on something, everything and anything around you is available. The world is a toolshed, and everything you hear, everything you see, and everything you feel is a potential tool.

I thought that it could be the perfect place for my choir to meet, but first, I needed some intel. Maybe it's the teacher in me, maybe the parent, or just an innate moral compass, but my first thought was, "I need to find a way to get the kids up there without walking them through the bar."

Before I even discussed the idea with one person, I began to survey the property, as if I were thinking of buying the place. Eventually, I noticed a door that looked like the entrance to a house, on an entirely different street, yet still attached to the bar. No one ever used this front door. After more investigation, I realized that if I could enter through the front door, I could head straight upstairs to the function hall.

But, of course, I couldn't do this alone. Eventually, I'd need to ask for help. I've never been afraid to ask for help. Why should you be? In order to get or use something, you have to ask, right? Simple math. So I asked one of my closest friends, Keith, who was on the board of directors for the Protectors Club. He seemed to like the idea and invited me to come and make my case in front of the board.

I went to the next meeting of the Board of Directors, and there I was, in a room, sitting in a chair, facing twelve white guys. If I had a dollar for every time I said that, I'd be rich. I explained that I was from Brockton, I knew the area, I knew the people, and I wanted to give back to my community somehow. I also informed them that I didn't have any money or anything to give them in order to use their space. I simply needed a place.

After some discussion, they allowed me to use the function hall, free of charge. The fire in me was ablaze. I was about to create my choir. Now, all I needed was the talent. In the amount of time that I had and without going door to door, all I could do was spread the word on Facebook and let the cards fall where they may. The entire intention of this choir was to do something for my city where no one had to pay to participate. I love watching kids enjoy being part of something bigger than themselves while learning along the way.

Music is my joy in life, but it can be more than just a source of joy for kids. Music creates the feeling of teamwork, confidence, and self-esteem, to name a few of the benefits. Making it free of charge was my way of giving these very valuable experiences to the children of Brockton. I wanted to use my skills, however small or big, to make a difference.

I ended up recruiting about twenty kids. All parents had to do was drop their kids off at noon. I would provide lunch (pizza), and pickup was at 2:00 p.m. Simple.

It went well for about three months. After three months, it happened. I call it the curse of Brockton Box. If you are from Brockton, you know exactly what I mean. The Brockton "Box" is something the locals like to say when someone from Brockton moves out and somehow gets sucked back in. It happens more than you know. Generally, people are happy to see a Brocktonian get out and make something of themselves, but when things don't work out, as they sometimes don't, they always come back. I know this from personal experience. I've left Brockton numerous times and returned just as many for a variety of reasons, some controllable, some uncontrollable.

In certain environments, no matter what you do, you simply can't make people do the right thing. Gradually, the kids began arriving fifteen, twenty, thirty, forty minutes late, until it became absolutely ridiculous. There was no rhyme or reason for the kids not to be there; however, the parents always were ready with an excuse, and this bothered me. At that point, I knew I had lost. From there, one by one, kids began dropping out.

I still have a hard time dealing with the fact that even when offered something educational, free, and simply great for kids, some parents still couldn't get out of their own way, or worse, out of their own kids' way. But, alas, you can't make people do anything. I can say with confidence that I gave it my best shot, and I believe the kids enjoyed doing what we did and received value from it. It got to the point where I couldn't chase people and drag them in for something I was doing out of the goodness of my heart. Eventually, I had to end the program.

At the end of the day, I feel like this, too, was one of my biggest accomplishments in life so far, even though the result may seem, to some, like it was a failure. I put my all into that choir, I did my best, and I showed up with everything I had to offer. To me, that's success. Someone once told me to stop trying to win the war and focus on the battle at hand. I won that battle. You can choose to seek all the experts in distant lands for all the answers, or you can choose to believe that everything you need is already inside you.

There are many reasons people decide to enter the teaching field. Some enter because they enjoy working with children, others because they like being off during the summer months, and still others because of their love for a particular subject. Although all these reasons are valid, my reasons are much simpler. These experiences confirmed my desire to teach and gave me the confidence to know I could do it. The bottom line is that I love kids and enjoy working with them. My desire to make learning a positive experience for the kids has only increased with time.

Because, ultimately, using everything leads to self-empowerment, and that is the only type of empowerment that counts. You don't have to wait for someone to give you permission, or a grant, or a job, or a way forward, or even to show up to rehearsal. You make your own choices, make your own moves, and reap all of the rewards from it. But you also live with the outcomes. No excuses. By using everything, you can empower yourself, take the action and the risks, and achieve the result you want.

7

REIMAGINE YOURSELF

"Happiness is when what you think, what you say,
and what you do are in harmony."
~ Mahatma Gandhi

For most of my life, I believed that people reimagined themselves in reaction to a frustration in their life. (Unless you're a pop star, in which case you shed your identity when it no longer remains profitable.) And that's how I thought of reimagining yourself—like a snake, squirming out of its skin. I thought I would start out in one version of myself, molt for a little while, then come out brand spanking new on the other side. But, looking back on past years, I realize that isn't true.

Reimagining yourself isn't something with a start time or an end time. It's a constant, proactive process of aspiring to be more than who you are today, and constantly reforming the image of who you are in response to your surroundings, hopes, and dreams. As part of that process, I've found that with each step along the way, I needed to re-examine what brought me here, to continue to ask myself if the choices that got me here are pushing me forward, or if they're weighing me down.

I received my bachelor's degree in music from Bridgewater State University in January of 2013, just two years after I enrolled. Many doubted that I would do it. I actually went to the same university in 1996 straight out of high school and flunked out my first year. I tried again in 2001 at a community college in Fort Pierce, Florida, but that was short-lived as well. After one semester, I realized I still wasn't ready to put in the work at the college level, and I withdrew.

When I went back to college after detox in September 2010, it was the result of reimagining myself while I was in the detox center. I announced to my friends and family that I was changing, that I was going back to school to pursue my dream of becoming a music teacher. I got a lot of positive feedback, but those weren't the loudest voices. The loudest voices said, "No one will hire a black guy with a felony." "Are you sure this is what you want to do?" "Is this what you truly want to do, or is this something you are just doing for your mom?" "Is this your dream or your mom's dream?"

When I think back to all the people who told me I was a fool for pursuing a teaching career with my record, I have to say, "Thank you. Because of you, I was given the drive to be better than what I was."

Though some of my drive is a personality trait, being doubted just reinforced it. Being doubted and undermined made me more determined to do better than they thought I could. Without these doubters, and without the experiences in my past that made them doubt me, I wouldn't be who I am today. I'd be a less driven, less satisfied, more settled version of myself. Someone who never would have challenged himself, someone who never would have left his little angry bubble. Someone who never would have become as independent as I am now. Someone who might not have ever accomplished his dream of being a music teacher.

Their doubts, while hurtful, did make sense. I was never the type of guy who seemed like he would succeed in college. In fact, I'd already fucked it up twice before. That's why going back to school required me to reimagine myself, even if I didn't consciously realize it yet. At the same time, going to college as an adult was the only way that I was ever going to finish.

I was not ready for college right after high school. I was too immature and I had neither the discipline, the motivation, nor the courage to apply myself in an educational environment. Going back as an adult, I felt that I had attained these traits. Still, college posed a unique set of challenges for me. Although all of these challenges were surmountable with persistence and preparation, it was important to enter my experience as an adult learner with open eyes and a plan, and that's what I did. But that would have never cut it without fuel for my fire. The death of my mother provided the gasoline I needed to accomplish my goal. But I was still afraid. I didn't think of myself as the type to be able to survive college.

Reimagining myself meant I had to get out of the mindset that I wouldn't be successful in obtaining my degree. I had to forget about high school and the challenges I'd had. I had to stop worrying about how much I would stick out or feel out of place in a classroom filled with students much younger than I. This was the new me. All of these fears were completely understandable. Of course, I experienced self-doubt, but persistence and an eye on the ultimate goals—a degree and an opportunity to inspire kids—helped to keep me going.

When I met with my advisor, Sarah, she kept it as real as anyone could. I remember her telling me that this was not going to be easy, especially as a returning student. It was going to take a huge time commitment, and as long as I stayed focused on my goals, I would make it. She laid out a two-year plan that would somehow allow me to complete four years of school in two years. I literally loaded up and registered for eight classes per semester. This was the maximum amount of credits that one could legally take within a semester. Was I absolutely nuts? Apparently, I wasn't, because I did it. By attending every semester—fall, spring, and summer—for two full years,

I completed my schooling with a BA in music in 2012 and made the dean's list every semester. I walked across the stage with my mother's picture in hand in January of 2013. Proud of myself does not even come close to describing the sense of accomplishment that it gave me.

My academic performance was stellar throughout my adult college career, which surprised even me. For the first time in my life, I experienced what it was like to receive an A. For many, that may be nothing; for me, it was a total transformation. The shift in my thought process was simple: bad grades would only make my experience last longer, possibly requiring me to repeat classes, and I most certainly did not want to waste my time or anyone else's. But what defined a good or bad grade for me largely depended on my goals, and I had goals.

This may be obvious to some, but again, I speak from experience, and I seriously didn't know this or care to know it before my education actually mattered to me. Broken down by letter grade, a student with all A's can expect to earn a 4.0, all B's to earn a 3.0, and all C's to hit the 2.0 mark. GPA is calculated over a student's collegiate career by adding the resulting grades of classes together to gauge academic performance. As I write this, I can't help but remember a time when this was a foreign language to me. I think about how lost I was and how far I've come. When I was a kid, as long as it wasn't an F, I was good. But this time, I strived for so much more than that.

I was purposeful, responsible, and intentional about everything that had to do with my education. A big part of that was simply going to class, no matter what. And if I did have to miss class, I notified the professor as soon as I knew I was going to miss the class. Again, simple, but not for me (during this time). I took notes and engaged with the material, the faculty, and my classmates. I even dragged Steve Siagel into my madness. Steve and I spent MANY late nights in his office of Siagel Productions. We analyzed symphony after symphony as part of my homework. Can you imagine analyzing the first few pages of a symphony, accounting for every single note, explaining every accidental and every progression? I can, and we did. Steve, I love you for that and it meant the world to me, and my grades are the proof. I was every teacher's pet and loved every second of it. I made myself matter to them. I was honest about my intentions and my endgame. Not only did I matter to them, I mattered to my daughter, who was only two years old.

At the end of every semester, music majors had to perform in front of a panel of our professors. This performance decided whether you moved up a level or remained where you were when you got there. The day after this audition of sorts, there was a mandatory concert that was open to the public. You basically now had to show the entire music department your progress or lack thereof. It was a big deal. At one of the concerts, my daughter Zoe was there. I brought Zoe to every concert, and at times, even brought her to class when I had no other choice, so the entire music department knew who Zoe was.

The room was silent as I finished singing Sarastro's Bass Aria, "O Isis and Osiris," from *The Magic Flute*. It ends on a very low note. The kind of note that makes everyone afraid to be the first one to clap in case it isn't over. My daughter, being so young, was probably wondering why the room was silent, so she yells, "Daddy, are you okay?"

The place roared with laughter. So while I felt GREAT about one of my best performances, my daughter also made me feel that I matter. The beauty in all of this is that no one forced me to do anything I was doing at the time. I had made a choice and it was my choice to be present and give my all to my education, and I reaped the benefits.

Reimagining yourself is an ongoing and continuous activity of reflection and choice, rearranging your priorities, reframing your vision of the good life, and uncovering a new sense of being alive. Reimagining yourself is a lifelong process that you need to be continually engaged in to stay vital, fully alive in the present, and hopeful for the future.

I've always been great with short-term goals. In fact, I prefer them. Work my butt off for a few months to reach a goal? I'm down with that. I'll give up a social life, downtime, spending money, eating yummy food, whatever it takes, for the short-term. Long-term goals, uh, not so much.

Despite this preference for pretty immediate gratification, on this return to college, I did everything I could to follow through with this long-term goal. In this learning process of motivating myself to follow through with longer-view goals, here are a few steps that helped me to stay focused and on track.

I found that it helped to simply remind myself that I was in charge. Many times, when the going gets tough, we begin to feel like the choices we made (sometimes long ago) are not our own. Sometimes we must remind ourselves that we are the ones who originally set this goal. It's a good way to rev the engine.

I saw pretty quickly that I had to get serious if I wanted to complete my goal, stop staying out late so often, and learn to organize my time and resources far better than I had been. I had to trade late nights with my friends for late nights with textbooks.

When I was frustrated about what felt like a lack of movement toward my goal, I sat down and made a list of the steps I had already reached, and the results of those steps. I was almost always surprised at how much I'd produced. This clarity helped in releasing those feelings of frustration. Taking the time to have these talks with myself helped to reinvigorate me to renew my focus and encouraged me to continue. To follow through with a long-term goal, we have to have solid reasons that make sense to us. That said, goals aren't set in stone. Like everything in life, it's good to approach them with flexibility and open-mindedness.

If you can't successfully remind yourself of your initial reasons for going for the goal, and get re-ignited about those reasons, then it might be time to reassess. Only you can decide what is best for you, and the answer can change over time. It's so important to give ourselves permission to go for goals with full-on focus and gusto, or to change them, or put them aside for a while, or whatever else we decide is right at that time.

Of course, because reimagining yourself is a constant process, college wasn't the first time I did it. In 2011, while almost done with my BA at Bridgewater State University, I was hired as an after-school counselor at the Neighborhood House Charter School in Dorchester, Massachusetts. I viewed this as a step toward my ultimate goal of teaching music, and made sure that the NHCS was fully aware of my musical talents. Once they knew, they wanted to capitalize on the situation. Within two weeks of being there, I was giving after-school music instruction, and I started a choir. During my first full year, I worked for the summer camp as a math assistant, and then finally, I found myself on the payroll as the full-time music teacher's assistant. I was a real music teacher!

Well, that's what I told myself, and when you are constantly trying to reimagine yourself, that's what it takes. You have to believe you are what you want to be. It's not just mumbo-jumbo. When you visualize your positive future, you'll have an easier time reaching that peak performance. I felt like a music teacher, so that's what I was. I had to live it if that's what I ultimately wanted to do. So, even though my technical title when I started was "after-school counselor," I made opportunities for myself in the music department, because that's how I thought of myself. Eventually, it worked, and my title matched my perception. But it didn't happen right away. I went through a process, and one that didn't get off to a great start. When I arrived for my first day, I got buzzed into the run-down schoolhouse. A seasoned secretary stood on the other end of the door with an aging Latino janitor with a gold rope chain and gold cross medallion dangling from his neck. They both just stared me down, looking more like the tough mothers I knew from prison than school employees. I was dressed to the T, fresh! Line up tight, dreadlocks well maintained. I like to call it Urban Preppy. It was my first day as a "music teacher," while technically an after-school counselor, so I had to dress to impress. I might have been working in the hood, but that didn't mean I had to look hood. I never wanted to be a statistic type of guy. I needed to stand out. What's cooler than a well-dressed music teacher, you ask? Nothing. I didn't have experience as a music teacher, but I knew this was my chance to get it, and I was ready.

That's when I first met Maura, the director of the Arts Department. She was a very tall, nice lady who seemed excited to meet me. She was white, which didn't surprise me, and I instantly realized that this gave me the advantage. A new, male, black teacher in an inner-city school, educated, clean, and ready to work. We were a rare breed.

Like unicorn rare. No, rarer. Like *black* unicorn rare. Who wouldn't like that? She was a rare breed too—the kind of teacher who commanded respect in the hood. Her classroom was clean and organized, and the kids' pleasant behavior in the classroom when I walked in proved that she was a power player.

She brought me around the school, showed me all the grade classrooms. We said a quick hello to some of the other teachers, and a few of them started a conversation, trying to get the scoop on the new guy. Eventually, we made it to the music room. My palms were sweaty and the back of my neck was hot, especially with eleven years of dreadlocks suffocating the top of my head and the back of my neck. Behind that imitation wood door was the only person who I needed to impress.

That person ended up being a woman named Karen. The look of disgust on her face was ten times worse than any face I got from the seasoned secretary and the Latino custodian. She tried to hide her outright anger and fear toward me behind a big smile, but that was about as effective as using torn nylon tights as a mask during a bank robbery. She shook my hand and said, "I've heard a lot about you."

Not "Hi!" not "Hello, my name is Karen," just, "I've heard a lot about you." At that moment, I knew exactly what this was going to be. She was totally threatened by my presence, and I could tell that she was going to try to prevent me from obtaining a role as a music instructor.

But I could not let Karen get in my head and deter me from my endgame. If I wanted to be a real music teacher, I would have to survive this. Unfortunately, I was now this woman's assistant and had to interact with her every day. In the past, I would have probably lashed out at Karen. But, part of reimagining myself meant that, no matter how dark my situation appeared or felt, I had to bring light to it. I had to bring forth change in myself by being the change. Whenever I felt the urge to succumb to petty fights, to passive-aggressivity, or even aggressive-aggressivity retaliating, I focused on the bright spots. I reminded myself that negative doesn't cancel out negative, positive does. As long as I remained true to myself and treated Karen with thoughtfulness, respect, and honesty, I couldn't lose.

And, perhaps in part because of my attitude, for all of my worrying, Karen never ended up being a real problem. But she did challenge me. And, as always, I responded to her challenges and used them to help me grow. She watched me closely and checked up on everything I did, so I had to make sure my stuff was together at all times. This made me a better teacher for sure, but it could have been a different outcome had I not gone into the Neighborhood House Charter School knowing that I likely would face these types of challenges. I did, after all, have a record with time served in jail, and, fair or not, when people see that, they're going to make assumptions about you and what type of person you are, and what your values are. I figured

I would be under the microscope when I first arrived. The fact is, I was still kind of surprised that I got the job. The Neighborhood House Charter School was the first institution to give me a chance, regardless of my past. I am forever grateful for that opportunity and experience. And it helped launch me forward.

While I was working at the NHCS, I was also teaching Zumba at The Dance Academy of Siagel Productions in Newton, Massachusetts, and MCing bar mitzvahs on the weekends. In June of 2012, a woman named Jodi approached me after one of my Zumba classes. She had been taking my class for some time and we had become friendly. She plainly asked, "Don't you have your degree in music?" to which I responded, "Yes."

She went on to tell me that the music teacher at her son's school was retiring, and I would be a perfect fit for this school. I gave her my information and she said to give her a day or two and she'd get back to me. The conversation was just as simple and as boring as that. Little did I know, it was the spark that was about to ignite my forward progress. Three days later, Jodi came back to me with a phone number. Fast-forward two weeks and two interviews, and I somehow had gotten myself a full-time music teaching position at one of the most prestigious schools in the country, just like that.

Once again, it was time to reimagine myself. This was no fire drill; this was the real thing. I was now a real-life, full-time music teacher at a real school. It was the biggest sense of accomplishment I'd ever experienced.

A lot of people like to say, "My past does not determine my future," and in theory, that's great, but fundamentally, that statement isn't true. I am who I am today because of every step that I have taken to get here. I am now who I am today because of every choice that I made and every choice that was made for me. My yesterday does determine my tomorrow, but only I choose how. And ultimately, that's what reimagining yourself is about. It's about applying your power to choose how your past shapes your future. You get to decide what the story is. You can look at your past, at what happened, at the mistakes you've made, and the person you were, and you get to choose whether you will get hung up on an error and never develop the ability to overcome what you've done. Or, you can choose to learn. You can reimagine who you are, who you want to be, and integrate those lessons and then use them to change.

My past either could have been a launching pad or quicksand. We all know of the homeless drug addict who had a rough childhood, and we also know about the mega-successful entrepreneurs who had equally rough childhoods. Both kinds of people had a choice to make, to use what they had experienced as a tool, or to be used by it.

When we constantly reimagine ourselves and give our gifts in support of what we truly care about, we feel energized, committed, and enthusiastic about everything we do.

We're led to believe that the big choices we make will determine whether or not we will lead a purposeful life—the work we go into, the awards we win—but it's actually the singular moments, the small, daily choices we make that will give us the confidence and strength to reimagine ourselves as we continually steer toward the full expression of our life's purpose. I believe that how we name and claim our purpose, how well we embrace our reason for getting up every single day, determines whether we look back later on the richness of our life— or suffer with regret.

ACKNOWLEGMENTS

MY MOUNT RUSHMORE

The journey of writing a book requires all kinds of support, both professional and personal. Professionally, I want to thank my book coaching and editing team: my book coach and friend Robin Colucci, and her son, and my editor, Dylan Hoffman.

Robin, our paths crossed by way of a quirky little town called Waltham. Within minutes of meeting, you reinforced an idea that had been fermenting in my mind for years. You instantly inspired me to finally open up about my emotions on such a public platform and free my mind from the burdens I've carried for what seems like an eternity.

Dylan, thank you for sharing your mom with me; she loves you dearly. You understood my story and you managed my writing with care, consideration, integrity, and honesty. You challenged me in a brotherly way, which made it easy for me to be vulnerable. Your magic is real, and so is your style. Stay fresh brotha.

I have many to thank personally, as I would not have become the person able to write this book without the support of some very key people.

Thank you to my Uncle Jeff and Aunt Linda for allowing me to move into your home in Port St. Lucie, Florida, when I made the decision to leave life as I knew it behind in Boston and to bring music back into my life. Your help and support made it possible for me to rediscover myself, again. Thank you to my beautiful, resilient, and smart children for your love and understanding. Daddy is not perfect, and I do not expect you to be, but know this: I will always be here to listen, laugh, cry, and do my best to help you navigate this crazy world. I love you all with every drop of my soul.

Thank you to my dad. I truly believe writing this book brought us closer, and in some weird spiritual way, Mummy is behind all of it. I will forever cherish the time we spent sharing stories throughout my investigation for clarity on my life. I learned so much from listening to you and hearing your side of my story. And you were right. I did have "one foot on the banana peel," and I always will. But now my other foot is firmly planted in life, like the flowers that everyone slows down to look at when they drive by your house. I'm manicured, facing the sun, and maybe one day, I'll find my own sunflower, like you did.

We were Mummy's favorite men, and she's proud of us. I love you.

And now, I conclude these acknowledgments with an Ode to the four people who have made such a profound difference in my life, that I refer to them as "My Mount Rushmore." For they are the ones carved in stone as my greatest teachers and greatest supporters to whom I am eternally grateful.

Lou Siagel, I can proudly say that I knew you for most of my life before you passed, and I've missed you dearly. Before I was even old enough to attend Boston Latin, you made me love the violin. I played for many years before you were actually my teacher, but you instilled an unidentified, different love that I have for my instrument still today.

What I miss about you more than your huge smile and the way you would say, "Hey, Greggy baby!" every time you saw me, was your philosophy of teaching music. The way you taught music and developed a chemistry between student and teacher. It wasn't enough for you to teach how to play notes on a stringed instrument, or teach music appreciation in any form, unless it was "meaningful." I learned from your passion for music, for teaching music. I loved the way you spoke from the heart, like a poet. I learned from you that teaching music was "different" than teaching other subjects, because while each student's contribution was essential, each student must be interdependent on one another to value the pursuit of a perfect performance. You didn't just teach music; you felt the beat of its heart to make us always feel life more deeply and meaningfully because of our experiences, camaraderie, training, and discipline to share an invisible communication together to make music. I will always remember how you enhanced my life with dedication, mentoring, and caring. Your magic lives on, and I will continue to share it with the next generation of musicians in your honor.

For centuries, the greatest thinkers have suggested the same thing: Happiness is found in helping others. Helping others may just be the secret to living a life that is not only happier but also healthier, wealthier, more productive, and meaningful. Thank you, Lou Siagel, for helping me.

Steve Siagel, you are my mentor, my teacher, my coach, my counselor, my friend, my oracle, and for lack of better words, kind of like my dad. You have helped me advance my career, been there for me during my darkest hours, and given me advice about life from your vast knowledge and higher expertise. As every good mentor should, you have always given me free will to take your advice into consideration, leading me but not imposing on me. Our relationship has grown with dedication, communication, and trust, and I cherish our time together. We have certainly had our differences, but the way we bounce back stronger than ever, every single time, from those differences is what makes you, Steve Siagel, one of my greatest mentors and best friends.

From the moment we met, you have given me advice, made me feel better about life, and set me on the right path. But really, the moment that best sums up who you are and what you mean to me comes from a visit my kids and I made to your house. Zoe was about two years old and you overheard her say, "Daddy, who's house is this?" I replied, "This is my boss Steve's house." I could instantly tell by the look on your face that you didn't like that shit at all. You pulled me aside and said, "Greg, we're friends, please introduce me as your friend." I was blown away by you at that moment—up until then, I'd never had a real friend. I will never forget that moment. Your mother, the amazingly lovely Bev Siagel, once said that our relationship was Beshert, meaning "inevitable" or "preordained." Beshert we are. Much love and respect, Steve.

And Gpop, thank you. For the longest time, I wasn't sure you even liked me. I remember, as a young child I was intrigued by you. You were so smart, intelligent, handy, and all-around awesome. What white Episcopal Priest with no children of his own has ever married a black woman with nine kids, adopted all nine, and raised them to be awesome, productive people? Without you, it would have taken a miracle to save that family. You have continuously given me the gift of honest evaluation. Having the strength to embrace my failures over the years has strengthened my resolve, and I owe a lot of that strength to you.

You've watched me mess things up over and over again, but you saw a spark in me, and a change in me, when my mother died that gave you a reason to trust that I could realize my full potential. Even when I didn't see what I was capable of, you did. You saw a future in me, even when I was struggling to get through the day. And you did everything you could to nurture that spark. Thank you for reaching out when Ma passed and I decided to go back to college, for offering the emotional and financial support that I needed at that moment. Without it, I don't know if I would have been successful. But more than that, that support helped close the gap between us, and that's what I'm thankful for most of all: your presence in my life.

And, finally, I've saved the best for last. To you, Ma, I pay homage. You have shown me how to be strong, focused, and level-headed, regardless of what the world thinks of me. You have taught me how to care for myself and those around me. You have taught me the importance of vision and constantly working toward one's dreams. You have instilled in me the desire and ambition to succeed in my own life while still prioritizing the uplifting all those who are around me.

Everything good in my life, past and present, is in some way, somehow connected to you. Even in your absence, you are with me, and I owe everything I am to you, my mother. I'm not sure why this happened, maybe it's because yellow has always been your favorite color, but I have always related sunflowers to you, and you to sunflowers. Since you've been gone, I see them at the strangest times and most perfect times. The most memorable time happened in September of 2019 when I walked into my new teaching job on the first full day of school. The moment I opened the door, there was a woman standing with a bouquet of sunflowers. It was as if she had been waiting, in that very spot, just for me. I almost shit my pants. Sorry, I know you hate when I swear. But my point is, you always let me know you are there. I can feel you. I can smell you. I can hear your heartbeat. You were my greatest teacher, a teacher of compassion, love, and fearlessness. When I saw those sunflowers, I felt fearless. Thank you, I needed that. If love is sweet as a flower, then you, my mother, are that sweet flower of love.

About the Author

Greg Fernandes is the Choral & Music Director at Dedham Country Day School in Dedham, MA where he also coaches flag football for the varsity and JV teams. Prior to that, Greg was the first black music teacher at Buckingham Browne and Nichols School.

Best known for his ability to teach and work with children of all walks of life and socioeconomic backgrounds, Greg founded the Brockton Community Children's Choir in 2011 and started the first violin ensemble at NHCS (a charter school Dorchester, MA).

A high energy and dynamic speaker, Greg presented at the Middle School Students of Color Conference in 2018.

Greg also continues his twenty-year long gig as the premier MC for Siagel Productions where he is best known for his ability to orchestrate a party, bar mitzvah, wedding, or corporate event where the youngest and the oldest person in the room have an equally good time.

Greg has a BA in music, and has played the violin since the age of three. He sang in a do-wop band, Sha-Boom that opened for the Temptations in 2002.

Greg is a member of NAIS (National Association of Independent Schools), NAFME (National Association For Music Educators), MMEA (Mass Music Educators Association). He lives with his three children in Massachusetts.

Made in the USA
Columbia, SC
11 March 2020